Most entrepreneurs start new [illegible] little or no guidance from experienced [illegible]pany began in the living room of the S[illegible]agers joined the company family as it gre[illegible]s and experiences of each as the enterpris[illegible]Chico, CA, firm began a program that resulted in our SunGard group reaching $900 million in revenues and 5000 employees. This is an American success story that could help any new business grow.

Bob Clarke
Retired Group CEO
SunGard Data Systems Inc.

This book is a "must read" for anyone wanting to start a successful business. It also contains lessons and stories that will help an established business thrive. Through the personal stories of twelve experts, over 150 lessons are presented to guide you to a successful startup. Very useful!

Jim Mann
Retired CEO of SunGard

Gary, I have to say how glad I was to find you on LinkedIn. I'd like to tell you how much I've appreciated knowing you and how much I admire you. You may not even realize this but you taught me a lot about people and business. I would not be where I am today without your mentoring, even though I'm not sure you knew you were doing that. I have a copy of Sitton's Axioms in a frame on my desk. With all sincerity, thank you for your friendship, kindness, wisdom, and plain old horse sense. The next time you're in SLC, I'd love to buy you a drink and thank you in person.

Bill Haight
CIO, Salt Lake City Corporation

I met Gary and Judy Sitton, when the Bi-Tech software product was proposed to our organization to address our business requirements, in 1986. After a very short period of time it became apparent this Team maintained very high standards for themselves and their employees. Working with Gary and the entire Bi-Tech organization has been very inspirational and one of the most rewarding professional/personal experiences.

Our organization continued to be viewed as one of their most valuable clients before their success and after their success. This is a direct result of the leadership style Gary Sitton maintained with the entire Bi-Tech organization.

At a time when there were very few women in executive management and technology, Judy Sitton was inspirational and has had a very positive impact on the development of my executive management approach and style with both my consulting clients and colleagues. The test I have used prior to initiating most difficult conversations has been, "how would Judy Sitton handle this conversation?" I will always appreciate the leadership style, kindness, compassion, and professionalism she demonstrated.

Susan G Bostick
Vice President – Gartner Consulting
(Formerly Accounting Systems Manager – Solano County)

# Fire Up Your Startup and Keep it Up

**FIRE UP YOUR STARTUP AND KEEP IT UP**
**LESSONS FROM TWELVE BUSINESS AND ENTREPRENEUR EXPERTS**



*iUniverse books may be ordered through booksellers or by contacting:*

*iUniverse*
*1663 Liberty Drive*
*Bloomington, IN 47403*
*www.iuniverse.com*
*1-800-Authors (1-800-288-4677)*



*ISBN: 978-1-4917-4828-2 (sc)*

*Library of Congress Control Number: 2014918531*

*Printed in the United States of America.*

*iUniverse rev. date: 01/12/2015*

# Fire Up Your Startup and Keep it Up

Lessons from Twelve Business and Entrepreneur Experts

W. Gary Sitton, PhD

# Contents

# Foreword

According to the US Small Business Administration (SBA), a third of all startups fail within the first two years, and almost 60 percent are doomed to fail by their fourth year. And this is for seasoned entrepreneurs. First-time entrepreneurs have only an 18 percent chance of succeeding.

But you are ready to strike out on your own. You are done working for someone else, and your idea is amazing. You catch the entrepreneurial bug and are determined to be successful.

Most small businesses get started this way. Companies are created without any regard for market share, human resources, business strategy, customer service, or a sustainable revenue model. You become the CEO and are also the person that hires employees to run all the needed departments.

Gary Sitton surrounded himself with people willing to work hard and share their expertise. This is what successful startup entrepreneurs do. They leave their egos at the door and determine the best person for a specific job. They are good listeners and great communicators—and they are flexible, keeping an open mind to what works and what needs to be eliminated. Gary has all of those qualities and many more. I know because he is a dear friend of mine.

To understand all the parts of a startup, this book is an excellent resource. Gary, his amazing wife, Judy, and the cast of authors present you with a step-by-step manual of insights to drive growth. Personal stories of twelve business experts are woven into a tapestry of lessons that can help any entrepreneur start, grow, and run a successful enterprise.

Topics selected form the foundation of all successful business endeavors, from marketing to human resources, customer service to employee relations, and so much more. In addition, CFO duties, research and development, startup funding, acquisitions, global sourcing, project management, social media, and the virtual company are key topics of the book. While this work is oriented to the technical startup, its lessons speak to a much larger audience. And they make it seem simple and fun.

As you read this book, you will achieve what many entrepreneurs lack: passion, kindness, emotional intelligence, and connection. This information is a road map to success.

It is with great pleasure that I write this foreword. I am truly honored, and I hope you find this book as enjoyable and enlightening as I did.

Very best,
Marsha Petrie Sue, MBA
President, Communicating Results, Inc.

## About Marsha Petrie Sue

As a former corporate executive, Marsha now owns Communicating Results, Inc., a company she founded in 1992 with her husband, Al. She is a professional speaker, author, and executive coach working with clients around the world. She dares people to take personal responsibility for their choices, successes, and lives. Marsha is an original, one-of-a-kind professional speaker and author. Whether Marsha is dealing with employee relationships, increasing productivity, or pumping up sales, her guiding principles bring energy and fun to any meeting or event.

Her clients include small and large corporations, associations, healthcare institutions, and multilevel marketing companies. As a former corporate executive of a Fortune 100 company, Marsha understands what it takes to improve productivity and profits.

She is a best-selling author of *Toxic People: Decontaminate Difficult People at Work Without Using Weapons or Duct Tape* and also *The Reactor Factor: How to Handle Difficult Work Situations Without Going Nuclear.* She is also the author of several other resources, including the award-winning book *The CEO of YOU: Leading YOURSELF to Success.*

In addition, she volunteers her time to outdoor conservation projects, women's safety and leadership training programs, special-needs children, and wounded warriors in the outdoors.

# Preface

Entrepreneurism takes courage, or ignorance, and certainly passion. Not all of us have interest in identifying a problem, much less deciding to solve it. Fewer still set out to do so and make a business of it. This book is designed to offer insight to those who see problems as opportunities, seek to diminish ignorance with advice and experience, and apply their passion to what they love: solutions, challenges, and creation that leads to success.

America is not doing a very good job of encouraging startups, and the "common core" isn't helping (Zhao 2012). This book is a collection of presentations by guest lecturers in a graduate-level course titled Technical Startups. The class was offered in the 2014 spring semester at California State University (CSU), Chico. A similar class was offered ten years earlier, in 2004. This work would be an effective textbook in any postsecondary institution offering courses in entrepreneurism.

When I was asked to offer this course by Larry Wear, department chair of Electrical and Computer Engineering, I stipulated two requirements. First, the class was to meet at 6:00 a.m. on Tuesday and Thursday; second, free rein on guest-lecturer selection was required. While the university was not pleased with the 6:00 a.m. request, Larry went to bat for me, and both these requirements were met. If you've ever run your own business, you know why 6:00 a.m. was requested.

We ended up with twenty-five registered students, mostly electrical engineering, computer engineering, and computer science majors. Two dozen Krispy Kreme doughnuts and coffee were used to entice the students to attend each session. Five of the students were registered as "audit"; only one of them showed up consistently. We averaged twenty students per session.

***Lesson: We tend not to perform well if we don't have some skin in the game.***

Most of the guest lecturers would be considered "penny millionaires," having amassed less than $100 million. Most of them have started and sold multiple businesses, primarily in the technical sector; however, many of the concepts identified in this work will transfer well to other sectors.

The instruction to the guest lecturers was quite simple: "Make sure your presentation includes knowledge you wish you had received before you went into business." The textbook for the class was *Beyond the Pale*, a wonderful little book written by Ken Grossman (2013), president and owner of Sierra Nevada Brewing Co., located in Chico, California, and Mills River, North Carolina. This book chronicles "a company philosophy that emphasizes sustainability, nonconformity, following one's passion, and doing things the right way" (inside hard-copy leaf). It is also an amazing story of intellect, courage, hard work, dedication to quality, frugality, and some food for thought when considering a partnership.

There are several important aspects of running a business; I wanted to invite guest lecturers who would give the students a candid, field-tested introduction to the most critical aspects. Throughout these chapters, "Lesson" comments are inserted; these are compiled in appendix 2. Appendix 1 is designed to give helpful information for those businesses that find it necessary to conduct demonstrations of their products and services. This book is not written in a classic academic style but rather conversationally and human, just like the lectures.

The attempt here is to go beyond the usual "how to run a business" book and transcend the integral parts and concepts that can lead to a successful enterprise, focusing on the "why" as well as the "how." The reader is taken from a successful startup, through growth and, ultimately, acquisition. Marketing and sales represent the most important aspect of growth. No company excels without understanding the critical role played by human resources. Customer service and employee recognition are the fuel that fires a successful firm. The research and development chapter is rife with wit and great wisdom. International commerce is a focus, along with a very atypical presentation by a CFO. Technical enterprises must understand the importance of project management. Finding *new* opportunities and business realities are additional food for thought. Global sourcing and funding for a new enterprise are critical endeavors. Social media and the virtual company are a *huge* part of today's landscape. All these topics, and many more, are represented in the work that follows.

In each chapter, there's a common thread that, when woven together, provides a fabric rich in experiences, lessons, and examples of success for those entering and continuing to thrive in the world of commerce.

## Some Student Comments

> "In college, it is rare to find a course that has the capacity to combine entrepreneurial theory and real-life experience so seamlessly. Gary has assembled a series of all-star guest speakers. They shared their uncensored, firsthand knowledge of the world of technical startups. All this to help us, the students, avoid undue hardships, and to foster the next generation of technical entrepreneurs. It's the best damn class I've taken, period." —Charles Pooler (2014 student)

> "The wide variety of speakers, experts in their fields and disciplines, offer up unique perspectives and valuable insights that are often lost in more conventional discussions of business. Instead of leaving the audience with a large amount of facts and figures to sort through, the key elements of successful business practices are brought to light and emphasized." —Emily Parisi (2014 student)

> "I took Gary's class in 2004; it was a milestone in my path to founding and running my software company. Guest speakers who really walked the walk came in and inspired us to shoot for the stars, while providing real-world advice that I could immediately apply to my startup idea. All of a

sudden it clicked that I could reach beyond my computer science degree and actually start and run companies for a living! To this day, I remember and apply many of Gary's philosophies and ethics to my own company and continue to experience success as a result of that. I cannot thank Gary enough for completely volunteering his time and effort into giving back and developing the next generation of entrepreneurs." —Robert Strazzarino, president and CEO, Student Scheduler (2004 student)

# Acknowledgments

This book is dedicated to the fantastic group of guest lecturers who delivered amazing presentations to my 6:00 a.m. class. In addition to giving me the go-ahead to include their chapters, they generously shared their notes and PowerPoint slides so the draft-form chapters could be created. Each presenter had full editing rights to his or her chapter. The mix of personalities and topics was unique and inspiring. In addition, each presenter edited the entire manuscript and made great suggestions to improve the finished product.

Marsha Petrie Sue and Bay Barnett are both accomplished authors who devoted many hours to editing this work. In addition to the grunt work of line-in, line-out edits, they provided sage advice to a first-time author. This work would not have been presentable to a publisher without their generous tutelage.

Thanks are due to Larry Wear for coercing me into offering this class and going to bat for me with the administration to have the doors unlocked at 5:50 a.m. Also, a big shout-out goes to the students; they were a wonderful mix of US and foreign students, smart, energetic, and eager to learn from experienced professionals. It was wonderful to see them clamor for the presenter, after each session concluded, to extract just a little more information. It is hoped that every one of them goes on to experience the great joy of owning a company.

Jessee Allread also helped immensely. His edits and suggestions on the preface were spot-on. Daren Otten was also exceptionally helpful in suggesting the addition of a chapter road map, plus many other amendments that improved the entire work.

Bill Lane must also be thanked. Were it not for his bringing me under his wing, I likely never would have received a PhD, been a professor for seventeen-plus years, started a company, or written this book. It is amazing what a small act of kindness can accomplish.

Special thanks must go to James Bennett, who wrote nearly his entire chapter for me. I must say, run-on sentences and all, his chapter is my favorite. His wonderful wit is coupled with many very insightful observations from his thirty-year career.

Thanks are also extended to my daughter, Holly. As said in the first chapter, she is the most creative member of my family. She put together all of my PowerPoint slides for the class, and they definitely passed the "gee whiz" and "so what" tests.

Finally, thanks must be given to my wife of forty-seven years, Judy. In addition to writing her own chapter, she has edited and read every word many times. As is her nature, she calmly and respectfully made suggestions that greatly improved this work. She also excused me from several domestic duties while I toiled away on the manuscript. I can get back to taking out the trash now; however, I think I may like to write another book, perhaps on virtual project management.

# Chapter Road Map

This book tells the personal stories of many who have learned much, often through hard knocks, while living the American dream. These stories speak to the many challenges and opportunities faced from startup to exit. While it is suggested that the entire book be read, it is designed for use by those seeking guidance around topics that have particular, timely relevance. Depending upon where one is in a business cycle, some topics may be more relevant than others. I wish I had read this book before I started my company—and then kept it as a reference source while my company went from a mom-and-pop shop to a $30-million-per-year enterprise. After reading the book, the reader is encouraged to keep it around as a reference guide. If this book helps entrepreneurs be successful, my primary goal is achieved. Many of the challenges and opportunities addressed in this work are listed below, along with reference to applicable chapters.

| **Challenges/Opportunities** | **Chapter (bold most applicable)** |
|---|---|
| Finding your niche | **1**, 6, 9 |
| Most productive development environment | 1, **5**, 7 |
| Finding good employees | **1**, 3, 5 |
| Pirating your clients' employees | 1 |
| Strategies for economic downturns | 1 |
| Forming a user group | 1 |
| Finding time to develop software | 1 |
| Acquisitions | 1, **6**, 7 |
| International commerce | 8, **10** |

# 1

# Birth, Growth, and Acquisition of a Software Company: 3:00 A.M. Wake-Up Call

W. Gary Sitton

I was born in Chico, California, in 1945, lived in Chico until age ten, and then moved to Willows, California. I held various jobs: for example, cow milker and farmhand on a dairy ranch, and box boy for a local market (called courtesy clerks nowadays). During my junior year in high school, we moved to Modesto, California. The middle of my senior year, we returned to Chico. My family life could be accurately depicted as somewhat dysfunctional. My father was an alcoholic and left the family when I was twelve. He was a mean drunk and never related well to my older sister, Elaine, or me. We were high-fiving when he left. My mother supported us as a grocery-store clerk and secretary. My sister always signed my report cards so my mom would not know what a terrible student her son was. I'm not sure why Mom never asked to see one; maybe she knew.

I graduated in 1963 from Chico High with a remarkable cumulative GPA of 1.6. I didn't like my teachers, didn't like the classes, and was a bit of a loner. The main reason I graduated was that my history teacher, Mrs. Price, lost her grade book, so they gave me a "C" in the class. The only math class I took was Algebra 1, in which a "D" was given to maintain my eligibility to play football. When I met with the high-school counselor, he said trade school was my best option because he doubted the service would take me due to two knee surgeries from football injuries.

Upon graduation, I got a job as a stevedore with Valley Motor Lines in Chico. During the summer of 1963, a friend of mine said he was going to take the ACT and apply to Chico State. He suggested I join him. I decided to take the test, did well on it, and was admitted as a probationary student. My stevedore job supported me throughout my undergraduate work. By the middle of my sophomore year, the remarkable GPA of 1.6 had been reestablished. A letter from Don Gerth, dean of students (later to be the longest-serving president of CSU, Sacramento), said I had one more semester to keep him from sending my information to the draft board. I was adrift, with no real direction.

I made the decision to take a computer science class in the spring, 1965, titled Assembly Language Programming. In the first several weeks, I thought I had finally found something I liked and for which I had an aptitude. Then my father died, my apartment burned down, I had an emergency appendectomy, and I thought I had gotten a girl pregnant (turned out not). I managed to pull Cs in my other classes; however, I had fallen too far behind in my computer science class.

## The Epiphany That Changed My Life

Knowing there was no way I could pass the computer science class, I went to see the department chair, Bill Lane, and asked to drop the class. He said no but added, "I will give you an Incomplete, and you can take the class from me in the summer." I told him I couldn't afford summer school, and he said to just attend the class, take all the tests, do well, and he would send in a change-of-grade card in the fall. I took the class, did very well, and fell in love with computer science. If Bill had not taken a chance on me, I suspect my life would have turned out quite differently.

***Lesson: Sometimes, taking a chance on someone pays off.***

Throughout the remainder of the summer, I purchased and studied every computer science textbook available; then, in the fall, I successfully challenged many remaining computer science courses. I understand "challenging" a class has become an arduous process; what a shame.

In the fall of 1965, I was taking Linear Programming from an inept instructor. I went to see Bill and told him, "I could teach the class better than that guy"; to which he responded, "Okay, next semester, you teach it." Gulp! Gulp! With this appointment, Bill put me on a path that would lead to a PhD and a seventeen-plus-year career as a professor. I had found my niche.

There was not, as yet, a computer science degree program at Chico State; that didn't happen until 1967. Once I found computer science, I took heavy unit loads and became a good student, even in classes I didn't like. My math background was sorely lacking, so I bought and studied textbooks for algebra, geometry, and trigonometry. After a semester of pretty intense study, I was able to get As in calculus. I had several units in business, so I graduated in that school in 1966, three and a half years from when I entered Chico State.

***Lesson: You'd be surprised what you can do when you've found your niche.***

After graduation, I entered the master's program and was teaching part-time in computer science. I had taken a few graduate-level classes as an undergraduate, so I was able to finish my master's in the spring of 1967.

When I was a sophomore, I had to take Psychology 1A as a general education class. I couldn't help noticing this gorgeous girl named Judy Carlson; she was a freshman. Judy came from an extremely conservative family, an only child. Her father was a civil engineer; her mother was a stay-at-home mom. Her family was much like the Cleavers in *Leave It to Beaver.* I rode a motorcycle, smoked cigarettes, drank beer, and boxed on the college team. I pursued her relentlessly, and we became engaged.

In the spring of 1967, I had my master's and Judy had her baccalaureate. Judy and I were married in June 1967 in Southern California. We had a one-and-a-half-day honeymoon on Catalina Island and began the drive back to Chico. In Selma, California, our car dropped the driveshaft. I was due to start teaching summer school the next day. Calling Bill Lane, I told him I needed two things: he was going to have to teach my two classes the next day, and give me an advance to cover the rubber check we wrote to the mechanic.

We slept in the park and made it home late the next day. This was not as romantic as it sounds. Judy's idea of roughing it is no room service, so the honeymoon was not quite what she had envisioned. I went into my first class the next day, and ten minutes into the lecture, all the students stood up and applauded. Thoroughly embarrassed, I turned a very bright shade of red. When I met with my next class that day, I went through the entire lecture waiting for a similar outburst; nothing happened. Bill had choreographed all this the day before. He got me, good! Over the years, Bill and I greatly enjoyed getting each other's goat. He is a dear friend and a brilliant man, and he loves a good laugh.

## From the Air Force to a PhD

During that summer I received a notice to appear at Oakland Army Terminal for a physical exam to determine fitness to serve in the army. Going through the exam, my sweaty palms held letters from the two doctors who operated on my right knee. At the end of the exam, you are taken to meet one-on-one with an MD. When I showed him the letters, he asked what I was doing. "I'm a teacher," I responded. He asked where and what subject; my response, "Chico State and computer science." He said, "We are going to classify you 2B." I asked what that meant, and he said it's a special noncombatant classification in a critical-need area and to expect to be drafted within thirty days. Asking if that meant I would not be going to Southeast Asia, he replied, "No, it means we'll hide you behind a big rock" (exact quote).

With a lump in my throat, I raced back to Chico and took the nearest OTS (Officers Training School) exam for the air force. I figured if I had to do service time, I would rather be in the air force. I scored well on the exam, and they wanted to make me a pilot. So, back to Oakland Army Terminal to go through the same physical exam, this time for the air force. After the exam, I met one-on-one with another MD. He was the first African American doctor I had encountered. He said I had some heart irregularities and asked what I would be doing if I were not in the air force.

I told him I would be getting a PhD in computer science. He said, "Pack up your things and go home." I asked, "What about the army?" and he said he would take care of the army. I could have levitated back to Judy.

About a month later, a telegram arrived, telling me to appear at the Oroville Bus Depot in four days for induction into the army. I spent quite a bit of money on phone calls and finally got to talk to the air force MD with whom I had met. He told me it was a SNAFU (you know the acronym) and he would take care of it. One day before I needed to appear in Oroville, a telegram arrived saying, "Stand by; we are reviewing your case."

Judy and I stood by for one and a half years. Not that standing by was bad: I was an assistant professor and Judy was teaching second grade. We were managing apartments and had no rent; we had plenty of money. Finally I was reclassified "1Y," which is basically a "women and children first" classification. At last, we were free to get on with our lives.

***Lesson: Sometimes you need a bit of luck and a lot of patience.***

The search was on to find a place to pursue a PhD. The United States was a very unhappy place to be a university student in the late 1960s. The campuses were in turmoil over the Vietnam War. The University of Alberta in Edmonton seemed like a good alternative, primarily because the department chair called me directly and offered me a teaching job. In addition, I wanted to study under one of the originators of ALGOL 68, a computer language I thought would take over the world; it didn't.

***Lesson: Software languages come and go.***

The originator was assigned as my thesis supervisor. After a few months, I noticed some pretty bizarre behavior patterns with the man and asked the department chair, Dr. Scott, to be reassigned to a different supervisor. I was given to John Tartar, an electrical engineer; he was a great thesis supervisor.

**Lesson: Don't stay with a bad thesis supervisor or mentor.**

I took a class from the professor who was in charge of locating external examiners for all PhD theses. In class, he asked me what I thought of the class. I said it wasn't worthy of being classified as a graduate-level class; I had taken the same class at Chico in the undergraduate program. He was not pleased. My dissertation was titled "Microprogram Optimization Strategies," and a major part of it disproved a theory offered in a paper written by University of California, Berkeley Professor C. V. Ramamoorthy. Guess who got appointed as my external examiner.

I remember John Tartar calling me to the coffee shop on the morning of the exam, where I was to meet Dr. Ramamoorthy. I had a cup of coffee on a saucer, and you could hear the cup rattle from quite a distance. I sat down, and Dr. Ramamoorthy said, "Not to worry, Gary, I knew there was a problem with the theory when the paper was published." Whew! The exam lasted less than two hours; I made seven simple changes, printed ten copies, and headed to the bar. I was the first student to do a thesis on MTS (Michigan Terminal System), a text-processing system developed for the IBM 370.

**Lesson: When you are nervous, don't put the cup on a saucer.**

Judy and I greatly enjoyed our time in Edmonton. She was pursuing a master's in educational psychology, and I was enjoying all the hunting and fishing available in Canada. A couple of things stand out from my Canadian experience.

1. Judy was taking a tests and measurements class and needed to give someone an IQ test. She picked me; talk about pressure! What if my wife found out I was a dunderhead? Turned out fine, but it was a tense test.
2. Judy and I were sitting in the stairwell in my building, and the subject of having kids came up. After several salient points were made, I said, "You know, if we wait for the perfect time to start

a family, we never will." She agreed, and a month later, she was pregnant with our daughter, Holly. We had Holly on April 3, 1972, at the university hospital, and they charged us $5. That was refunded when they discovered we were both enrolled as students. It's interesting that when we returned to California, we paid $1,200 to have our son, Mark, in 1974.

***Lesson: The perfect time to have kids seldom appears.***

## Accounting Software

Returning to California was a joyous occasion for Judy and me. Those Edmonton winters are brutal. Judy returned to grammar-school teaching, and now, with my union card, the PhD, I was promoted to associate professor. Not long after my return, I was summoned by Gordon Fercho, the vice president for finance at CSU, Chico. He said all nineteen of the CSU campuses were having a huge problem with getting timely financial reports from the chancellor's office. He asked if I would be willing to write some software that could run on the individual campuses. It came to be known as AEL, Allotment Expenditure Ledger.

Because it was against system policy for a finance vice president to hire a programmer, I was hired as a budget analyst. It took about six months to get the system running. It seemed to solve the problem, and other campuses found out about it. Finally, the chancellor's office invited me to spend a summer documenting the software; then, many other campuses adopted AEL. I learned quite a bit about accounting while writing this software.

***Lesson: Treat each job as a training experience for your next job.***

About three years later, 1976, I was again summoned to Gordon Fercho's office. He had received word that the service bureau that provided accounting for the university foundation and associated students was going belly-up. He asked if I could write a basic accounting package and a payroll package for these two auxiliaries. I said I would try. I was introduced to Joyce Friedman, the CPA who was in charge of accounting for the auxiliaries. Joyce took me under her wing and gave me a crash course in fund accounting. It took about eight months to get the system up and running; it came to be known as IFAS, Interactive Fund Accounting System.

In the course of the development, I noticed that Joyce kept huge manual multicolumn journals. I asked if it would be okay if I took a little time to automate them, and she agreed. It took about a week to write, and it came to be known as TFS, Table Formatter System. Joyce was quite pleased, and we folded TFS into the basic accounting package. If only I had the vision to know what could have been done with spreadsheet software in the midseventies.

Mark Bookman, director of associated students, was looking to enhance his resume and move on to a bigger university. He asked me to ghostwrite an article for the *AOA Newsletter* describing the system. He told me to include, "For more information contact Gary Sitton at ..." When the newsletter was published, I received seventy-five written inquiries about the system.

I scheduled a meeting with Mark and Len McCandliss, the foundation director. After I showed them the seventy-five letters, Len leaned back in his chair and said (expletives deleted), in effect, he was not in the software business. He said, "Why don't we give you ownership of the package and you give us a percent cut for each system sale, as long as you use our hardware for your development?" Mark agreed. The entire meeting lasted less than ten minutes. They had an attorney, John Schooling, draw up the agreement, which stated that the auxiliaries would receive 50 percent of the first sale, 25 percent of the second, and 10 percent thereafter, until I was off their hardware. Our initial hardware platform was the HP 3000.

***Lesson: If you're going to sell software, you need clear title.***

## Our First Clients

The first system sale was to Whitman College, a prestigious liberal arts college in Walla Walla, Washington. They first bought the payroll system and then added the entire financial suite. I rewrote many parts of the system while installing at Whitman.

If you are wondering how I continued teaching and doing all the development, I had half release time as chair of the academic senate for two years, and I was able to cut back to one class per semester. As the business grew, my teaching time was only intersession and summer school; finally, I took leave without pay. It's important for the reader to understand that an IFAS implementation is a long and complex project, beginning with a lengthy RFP (Request for Proposal) and ending with a twelve to eighteen-month implementation cycle.

With the money we made from Whitman, we bought our own computer and got off the auxiliaries' system. Our next client was the foundation at Cal Poly, San Luis Obispo. Then we sold to Reed College in Portland, Oregon. My best students were hired as programmers, and we ran the business out of our A-frame house in the foothills of the Sierras. Most of the first hires are still with the company doing great work.

Those early hires were David Woodward, Todd Saylor, James Bennett, and Jen Liu. David was one class away from a double degree in math and computer science. Todd sat in the back of my class and said nothing; then, on the first midterm, he got the highest grade and even politely corrected one of my questions. James took database management from me, and while I was going through some complex algorithm, he asked, "How am I going to use this in my backyard?" (More on James later). Jen came to the United States on a tramp steamer from Taiwan. While his English skills were lacking, he was a brilliant programmer and tough as nails; he played rugby for the Taiwan national team. Jen went on to become a very successful consultant, but the rest of these guys are still with the company.

## Incorporation

In early 1981, we decided it was time to incorporate. We gave considerable thought to the name and came up with ABACUS, "Auxiliary Business Academic Computer User Systems." Very cute, right? Marge Fong Eu, secretary of state, sent us our incorporation notice on April 3, 1981. This happened to be my daughter's ninth birthday. Our logo was an abacus with the embedded binary equivalent of 1981, the year of our incorporation.

With $5,000 left in our savings, Judy and I went to Orlando, Florida, for an HP vendor conference. We had a very basic ten-by-ten booth with a trifold brochure on our system. We were somewhat taken aback when people would stop and tell us they had heard of ABACUS. Upon our return home, we found out why. A letter from the attorney for a company already called ABACUS greeted us, demanding that we cease and desist from using their name. Turns out they were in San Francisco and served not-for-profit clients, just like us.

Calling our attorney, Todd Petersen, we told him what we had received and that we didn't have the money to make a name change. He said he would do the work pro bono and asked me what the new name should be. Having given this name change no thought, I figured binary technology would likely be around for quite awhile, given that trinary technology never established much traction. So, in a five-minute phone call, the name Bi-Tech was proposed. This name stuck. Warning: Don't forget the dash. We sponsored a Little League team, and they put the name on the back of the uniforms without the dash. You could hear the parents say, "Does that say Bitch?" We kept our logo.

***Lesson: Don't rely on the secretary of state to search your company's name.***

Through the early eighties we continued to add clients and employees. Judy quit her teaching job and became executive vice president. At the request of Orlando Madrigal, chair of computer science after Bill Lane had moved on to dean, my tenure-track position was relinquished so they could fill my position with a new hire. We went through three painful remodels of the A-frame home, expanding it to nine thousand square feet, plus a tennis court and hot tub. We went through one winter where a sheet of plastic separated our bedroom from the outside elements; Judy never complained.

When we hired our seventeenth full-time employee, it was time to relocate to a "real" commercial property. The strain on the A-frame's plumbing system was considerable. And sadly, many of the programmers had designated trees that they would leave behind when we moved to the new location. Since I and three other programmers, James Bennett, David Woodward, and Gary Wolz, had pilot licenses and a plane to fly, we relocated to the airport. Our new address was 1072 Marauder, Chico, California.

One of the early strategies we employed to make our company strong was to only interview people with outstanding academic records. To interview, we required a 3.5 GPA or better; and we always reviewed the academic transcript. This requirement was relaxed once we were well-established and realized that GPA is not the only predictor of greatness. We even found people in disparate disciplines who excelled, for example, music, communications, and home economics.

We were always on the lookout for great employees. Every time I went into a local business, I would carefully watch the employees. On one trip to Toys R Us, I noticed an employee running through the aisles, checking prices and locating products; he never slowed down and had a wonderful demeanor with the customers. I pulled him over to the side and asked how long he had worked there and if he was also a student. He said he was a chemistry major and had worked there for two years. He was offered a job at Bi-Tech and became one of the most successful salespersons in the company. His name is Christian Meyer, and he is still with the company.

***Lesson: Always be on the lookout for a great employee.***

Throughout the course of our growth, we came to know many great people who worked for our clients. When I wanted to lure them to Bi-Tech, I would first go to their supervisor, tell the supervisor that I wanted to make a job offer, and ask if he or she was all right with that. I also said that if the person was on a critical project, I would wait until that project was completed to make the offer. With only one exception, all the supervisors gave me the go-ahead; however, some did ask that I wait until a project was completed. The longest wait was for Mike Carver, an exceptional accountant with many years of experience in implementations. We waited over a year to make the offer to Mike. Well worth the wait!

***Lesson: There's a right way and a wrong way to pirate your clients' employees.***

Many significant events occurred in the eighties and early nineties. We were experiencing tremendous growth, and we were starting to see some very large firms enter our market: PeopleSoft, Oracle, SAP, and AMS, to name a few. A major contributing factor to our growth was diversity. We expanded into large foundations, K–12 organizations, and municipal governments. We also rewrote the package to migrate from the proprietary HP 3000 platform to a UNIX-based platform. Some of our larger clients were National American Red Cross, Scripps Research, NOAA, Salt Lake City, University of Notre Dame, and Harris County, Texas.

***Lesson: Diversity of vertical markets can help you withstand downturns.***

## The User Group, Continued Growth, and Tragedy

We started a user group in 1985. We felt it was important to have the user group be completely autonomous, run by our clients. They named themselves BSNUG, Bi-Tech Software National User Group, pronounced "Bee Snug." We held spring regional meetings on both the East and West Coasts and a fall national meeting. The spring meetings would draw up a list of proposed enhancements to the package, and in the fall, each client would vote on the enhancement list. We would report on those we had completed, those we would complete, and some we would not complete. This was invaluable to the improvement of the package.

***Lesson: If you are going to have a user group, let the users control it.***

One of the best days of my life leading Bi-Tech was the day we became large enough to have a director of personnel. We were close to eighty employees. Kristi Bennett, James' wife, was appointed director of personnel. She was given only two directives: don't tell me anything personal about the employees and keep me out of jail. From that day forward, when someone would show up at my door with a personal issue, I would simply direct him or her down the hall to Kristi's office. One of the things I am most proud of is Bi-Tech never being involved in litigation of any kind. This is quite a statement for a company with two-hundred-plus employees and three-hundred-plus clients. Kristi and the quality of our other employees made this possible. Also noteworthy: Kristi kept me out of jail.

Although we were never involved in litigation, we had our share of angry clients. Judy was, by far, the best trainer on the package; however, when it came to solving a client crisis, she had a halo. I can't fathom the number of hours she spent on the road and on the phone with mad clients. The result was always the same: the problems were solved, the client calmed down, and Judy got to move on to the next crisis. Based on her contribution to Bi-Tech, they should have loge seating in heaven reserved for Judy. Over the years, I have observed that husband-and-wife companies either work great or not so well. We were lucky. I had limitations; she did too. To quote Rocky Balboa, "We filled gaps."

The growth of Bi-Tech created a dilemma for me. While I certainly enjoyed the revenue, I was spending most of my day doing software demonstrations, negotiating contracts, or talking to clients. My favorite part of working at Bi-Tech was developing software. The decision was made to alter my work schedule. From 4:00 a.m. to 8:00 a.m., I would write software; the rest of the day would involve my other duties. I set the alarm for 3:00 a.m. I never required much sleep.

Our daughter, Holly, was a great student, and ended up being admitted to Whitman College, where she selected physics as her major. That lasted one semester, and she promptly changed her major to English literature and started auditioning for plays. And I'm thinking, "Where did I go wrong?" When she went off to college, she asked me for any advice I had. I told her to learn Chinese. Wanting to please her dad, she signed up for Introduction to Chinese. After one semester, she called to tell me she received a gift of a "B-" in the class, and her professor said her pronunciation was the worst she had ever heard. Her professor told her to stick with theater.

Our son, Mark, was not a great student in high school; however, he was good enough to be admitted to CSU, Chico, where he majored in computer science and then switched to math. We had some wonderful math discussions until he took advanced calculus. I was left in the dust. In his junior year, he went to University of Colorado to complete a degree in applied math. As an undergraduate, he published a refereed paper on neural networks. He was accepted into the PhD program at MIT in cognitive neural science, with a full-ride scholarship.

In 1992, I asked Mark if he would like to take over Bi-Tech someday. He said, "No, too practical." After one semester at MIT with straight As, he took a plane from Boston to Chico and caught a cab to our house. Judy and I were in Houston courting Harris County. Mark committed suicide at our home, on January 23, 1998, at age twenty-three.

James Bennett, Aaron Johnson, and Holly met us at the Sacramento airport to give us the terrible news. It changed our lives forever. To this day we continue to ask why. I wish I could add a ***lesson*** here to help others avoid the same experience, but sadly, I can't. There is no lesson. No explanation. Only questions and the deepest sadness one can know.

I regret not considering Holly to take over Bi-Tech. She continues to work for SunGard today, answering RFPs. She worked for us for many years and was an outstanding trainer, help-desk person, installer, demo presenter, problem solver, and software/report writer developer. Most of her work was in payroll and HR, our most complex modules. For some very lucky reason, she got the good genes from my side and Judy's side. She is clearly the most creative member of our family. She also has Judy's "character antenna" and could spot a bad employee long before I could.

## Acquisition

Once I knew Mark had no interest in Bi-Tech, I began to toy with the idea of being acquired. I engaged the services of Geneva Capital Markets, and they assigned me to John Dorey. Judy and I prepared a list of requirements for the acquisition: fair price, improved benefits package, no merging of user groups, financially stable company, maintain the same software platforms, and Judy and I could stay on to run Bi-Tech after the acquisition. The first suitor was a guy out of New York. We had one meeting, and I couldn't see myself working for him; he was kind of snotty. We also had one meeting with PeopleSoft. They wanted to merge user groups, and they wanted us to adopt some software I was not willing to adopt; not a good fit.

***Lesson: If you are looking to be acquired, prepare a list of requirements.***

The third suitor was SunGard Data Systems. As Jim Mann, their CEO, put it, "we are a very acquisitive company." They owned many companies, mainly in the area of banking systems; we would be their first foray into a fund accounting company. There were a few meetings with Bob Clarke, who was to become my boss if we were acquired. We hit it off well. Reaching out to former owners who were acquired by SunGard gave very positive results. Both Judy and I felt that we had found a good fit. Their benefit package was better than ours; they had no interest in merging user groups or changing software platforms; and as long as you made your "number," they left you alone to run the company. For reasons I didn't know, after these initial steps, they simply stopped all contact with us. Judy and I were crestfallen and decided we would just keep Bi-Tech until we became too old to run it.

One year after we dropped off SunGard's radar, I received a call from Rick Tarbox, SunGard's acquisitions officer. He said to meet him in two days at the east Red Carpet club in Denver International Airport. He said SunGard was prepared to make an offer for Bi-Tech. I called John Dorey, and we made flight arrangements. I had no idea what to expect. I wondered what the document containing the offer would look like. We had finished a very successful 1994, with revenue near $30 million.

Rick Tarbox came into the private room we had arranged, pulled an envelope out of his pocket, and slid it across the table to me. On the back of the envelope, in pencil, were the words, "$x purchase price, $y earn-out in three years." I told Rick I would need to step out and talk to John Dorey. Outside, I told John that x was much, much larger than I was expecting. "What should I do, John?" He said go back and ask for one more million in earn-out. I did and Rick accepted it. The meeting lasted less than an hour.

I asked Rick why they decided to acquire Bi-Tech, and he said Jim Mann, at a recent board meeting, asked, "Whatever happened to that Bi-Tech deal?" The response was that they thought he had lost interest. He said he had not and to go make an offer. An interesting aspect of the acquisition was that I was offered $x upfront cash or $x in SunGard stock. If I had taken the stock, I would have tripled the money. Nothing like hindsight!

***Lesson: When given the option of money or stock, consult experts before deciding.***

The first employee we told was Bruce Langston, our vice president for finance. He would be a key figure in the due-diligence phase. We told the employees that we had some auditors coming in, SunGard due-diligence accountants. SunGard had acquired enough companies to have this down to a science. I recall it lasted less than two months. The due diligence went smoothly for the most part. There was a little drama over the "clear title" issue, but eventually CSU, Chico, cleared that up. Bruce was amazing during the due-diligence process—damn good CPA. Once the due diligence was completed, we moved on to negotiate the purchase agreement.

On my side was our acquisition attorney, Rob Wood. Rob is a Columbia graduate with a very successful law firm in San Francisco, an all-around great man. On the SunGard side was Frank Diehl. Frank was a handful, and we had some marathon conference calls during the negotiation. On one call, we were approaching the three-hour mark and I had to relieve myself. I didn't want to interrupt the discussion because it was at a critical point, so I used my wastebasket. Let me add that my door was shut.

So, on June 30, 1995, Judy, Holly, Mark, and I rented a suite at the St. Francis in San Francisco and waited for confirmation of the funds transfer to our Merrill Lynch account. We had Rob Wood and John Dorey with us. The transfer came through, and we went off to have a wonderful celebratory dinner. Rob Wood, who has a terrific sense of humor, presented Judy and me with the following resolution:

### Francis E. Diehl Memorial Conference-Call Award

KNOW ALL PERSONS BY THESE PRESENTS

WHEREAS, W. Gary Sitton (hereinafter referred as the "Party of the First Part") and Judy L. Sitton (also variously referred to herein and in accompanying documents

> and schedules as "Judy L. Sitton" or "Executive") have faithfully discharged their duties as writers, rewriters, editors, legal consultants, parents, mollycoddlers, and various other and sundry helpers and assisters of that certain, that most honorable Esquire, Francis E. Diehl (hereinafter sometimes referred to as the "Party of the Second Part," "Attorney Diehl," "Diehl Breaker," or "Turkey Butt").
>
> WHEREAS, the Party of the First Part has undergone grievous bodily embarrassment, including the lack of time to undertake even the most basic of human functions, and instead has conducted himself so as to at all times avoid upsetting, agitating, confronting, or even maligning said Diehl.
>
> NOW, THEREFORE, BE IT RESOLVED, AND WITNESSETH, that said W. Gary Sitton shall be and is hereby awarded this Certificate of Merit with Highest Distinction entitling said Sitton (hereinafter sometimes referred to as "Honoree") to a free consultation with said Diehl at a time and place to be mutually agreed.
>
> BE IT FURTHER RESOLVED, that in order that further embarrassing incidents shall not, do not, and need not occur, said Honoree shall be and hereby does this day receive a receptacle, to be henceforth referred to as "The Diehl Bottle" to be employed in faithful service.
>
> Presented this 14th day of July in the year Nineteen Hundred and Ninety Five.

With due diligence complete and the purchase agreement signed, Judy and I had the task of telling our two-hundred-plus employees and our three-hundred-plus clients. We rented a large facility and brought most of our employees to the meeting. When we disclosed that we were being acquired, the employees took it better than I expected. There was shock, of course; however, I also observed a sense of excitement. They liked the improved benefits package and they liked the idea of being part of a really large company. At that time, SunGard was the thirteenth-largest software services company in the world. When we sent the announcement to our clients, the reaction was mixed, with a clear "wait and see" tone.

We stayed on to run Bi-Tech for five years. Thanks to a very large contract with Harris County, Texas, we were able to make nearly all of our earn-out. One of the things that helped us get our earn-out was to give out "Judy and Gary Bucks," basically a replica of a dollar bill that indicated what it would be worth if we achieved our earn-out. Many of our employees received very large checks when we made it.

SunGard was very generous with its presidents, offering a substantial salary and stock options. I learned a great deal in my five years with SunGard. Bob Clarke was an excellent mentor. We went through a few painful hiring freezes, but we never were in a layoff situation. We managed to make our "number" each year and were always rewarded with a higher "number" the next year.

The budget negotiations were an interesting study in corporate America. We would bicker back and forth; then, at the eleventh hour, they would tell us what our "number" was to be. The main difference in philosophy related to staffing. When we owned Bi-Tech, we would ramp up for expected growth; SunGard's philosophy was, "Do the deal, then ramp up."

After Mark's death, I lost the "fire in my belly." Being at Bi-Tech was a blessing and a curse—a blessing because it gave me something to do and a curse because I knew I was not giving all that I should. Judy and I realized we needed to do something else. We retired in early 2000 and left Bi-Tech in the very capable hands of Aaron Johnson. Aaron had been groomed for five years and did a herculean job managing the very difficult implementation project at Harris County.

In addition to being brilliant and having wonderful people skills, Aaron has a wry wit that will make you belly laugh. Case in point: I was having a meeting with the officers and I brought up the term "Pickle Ball," a game somewhat like handball. None of the officers had ever heard of the term; I was surprised. I decided to ask the next person to walk by the room. It happened to be Aaron. I said, "Hey, Aaron, do you know what Pickle Ball is?" To which he answered immediately, "Something I avoid on the hors d'oeuvres tray."

Judy said this chapter should finish by explaining why our software package had such widespread acceptance. Certainly the enhancement lists drawn up by our clients had a very positive impact; however, the most important characteristic of the package was its flexibility. Being able to service K–12, municipal government, higher education, and private/public foundations with the same product was our salvation. Through very carefully crafting the core of the software, we were able to have the exact same software running at University of Notre Dame, The Cousteau Society, Salt Lake City, Orange County Office of Education, Scripps Research, and the American Samoan Government. If you went to any of these client sites, you would swear they each used different systems. This is because each client can cosmetically and functionally customize our standard package. We only had to install, update, maintain, and support one product.

***Lesson: Careful crafting can create a very flexible software package.***

Thus, we conclude this rather narcissistic chapter on me and Bi-Tech. Hopefully you found some helpful lessons among the ramblings. For others reading this, I sincerely hope that you can see the bridge to your business and maximizing success.

If your startup has to do demonstrations to prospective clients, you may find some useful information in appendix 1. Appendix 2 is a compilation of the ***lessons*** offered in this work.

# Marketing and Sales: It Ain't Golf and Martinis

Drake Brown

Drake Brown was educated at BYU-Idaho, Idaho State University, Golden Gate University, and Colorado State University. His first career job was as a sales representative at a division of 3M Company in Foster City, California. He also worked for Hewlett Packard Company in Mountain View, Cupertino, and Sacramento, California, before joining Bi-Tech Software Inc. in 1992. In 1995, Drake became vice president for sales and marketing at Bi-Tech. He retired from the software industry in 2011. In his encore career, Drake is the director of the LDS Institute of Religion, serving the students of both Butte College and Chico State. Drake also teaches Marketing 305 at Chico State. Drake and his late wife, Cindy, have five children. He enjoys waterskiing, riding dirt and mountain bikes, cycling, and triathlons. Among the many jobs Drake held to get him through college, the most interesting was breaking rank horses.

Drake is perhaps the one person most responsible for the sustained growth of Bi-Tech. His in-depth knowledge of marketing and sales, coupled with his work ethic and complete honesty, made him the MVP in our company. If students were going to form their own businesses, I wanted them to have a comprehensive introduction to marketing and sales. Drake's experience made him the perfect choice to convey the message.

## The Software Business Cycle

Drake begins by describing the business cycle for a software company. We start with the software development, focusing on client requirements; the three main aspects are functional, technical, and cosmetic. After development, we move to both alpha and beta testing. Now it's time to make the software available with a "general release" and version updates. The system is completed with documentation, required professional services, and required alliances with database, hardware, compilers, and drivers.

We now move to the marketing and sales part of the business cycle. Marketing includes advertising, trade shows, and data sheets. The sales part is comprised of prospecting, qualifying, presenting, closing, and negotiating. In comes the client with the purchase (hooray!), followed by support, training, and consulting. The software business cycle can be summarized by: build it, test it, release it, market it, sell it, and support it.

## Marketing and Sales—They're Different

Drake differentiates a marketing plan from a sales plan. The four key elements of a marketing plan are product, price, promotion, and place. The sales plan includes budget/quota, prospects, qualifying, closing, and negotiating. He points out how the world has changed in only a few years: now your product details are on the web, Yelp and other online rating systems are in place, and the successful company establishes and monitors its online presence.

As your company grows, the marketing roles take shape. The head of marketing is responsible for the strategic marketing plan, company positioning, marketing message, branding strategy, and corporate identity plan. Field marketing includes value proposals, rep training, identifying vertical markets, target identification, and reference programs. Product marketing involves packaging, stock presentations, product requirements and documentation, competitive assessment, pricing maintenance, and RFP responses. Channel marketing includes OEM (original equipment manufacturer) relationships, consultant liaisons, analyst liaisons, and alternate channel strategy. The final role is "Marcom" (marketing communications), which includes advertising, promotions, public relations, and trade shows.

***Lesson: Knowing all the roles of marketing will help you grow your business.***

Marketing has four main objectives: (1) Create buyer awareness; (2) Assess and determine market and product focus; (3) Manage and create business alliances to deliver a complete solution; and (4) Provide sales support material.

The sales process has five main components.

1. **Prospecting**: This involves cold-calling, trade shows, referrals from customers, referrals from businesses, and direct mail.
2. **Qualifying**: Evaluate the prospect's budget, discern if there is a good functional and technical match, evaluate the procurement process and time line, and identify the buying criteria and decision makers. This is where you need to ask lots of questions and listen very carefully to the answers. Acknowledge early on what you can and can't provide.

***Lesson: The earlier you can disqualify a prospect, the more success you will have.***

3. **Presenting**: This involves RFP (Request for Proposal) response, remote demonstrations, data sheets and success stories, and on-site demonstrations.
4. **Closing**: Discover each buyer's opinion after the demonstrations, plan to address each obstacle, and then address each obstacle.
5. **Negotiating**: Understand their motivation, help them understand your motives, identify deal killers, compromise on deal killers, and understand the entire picture before giving things up.

***Lesson: Selling is a process.***

Drake goes on to describe the very important "sales funnel." There are four parts to the funnel.

1. **Above**: These potential clients are identified as "suspects," with no clear time line; still qualifying and not included in the sales forecast.
2. **In**: Active prospects included in the forecast; they have a time line, and we are actively spending sales time and resources (demos, RFP, etc.).
3. **Best Few**: Well-qualified, RFP and demo complete; we have reason to believe that we have a 50 percent or better chance of winning, and the deal will close within six to nine months; we are on their "short" list.
4. **Done Deal**: We have been formally notified that we are the selected vendor; actively negotiating or waiting for board approval.

The last three parts of the funnel make up the sales forecast. As the company grows and collects year-over-year data, the sales forecast can become an extremely accurate predictor of future revenue. You will develop your own mathematical model, which is simply the percent in each of the last three parts of the funnel that become a done deal and the revenue associated with those prospects.

***Lesson: Become a student of the sales funnel and sales forecast.***

## Profile of a Great Salesperson

1. **Be a person with the ability to become a trusted advisor.** This same term is used by presenter Michael Reale; he identified the three steps to becoming a trusted advisor: vendor, credible source, and trusted advisor.

***Lesson: Trust is earned through honesty.***

2. **Learn how to listen, observe, and question**. Contrary to popular belief, the successful salesperson does not have a flashy presentation and the gift of gab. Rather, the successful salesperson spends a majority of time listening, observing the reality of what has been said, and asking questions so that additional observations can be made. It's all about learning.
3. **Be the person whose follow-up you can set your watch by**. Drake says, simply, "If you can't follow up on time with correct information, you're dead." Enough said.
4. **Be the person with great business judgment**. Do not rush to judgment. Never make a decision while you are emotionally engaged. Learn that it is much better to walk away from a deal where the fit is not good.

***Lesson: If the fit's not good, walk.***

5. **Be able to close on each conversation**. Before you hang up the phone or end a meeting, provide a verbal summary of what you think you understand. This will clear up any misunderstanding and can give rise to some important points that did not come up during the conversation.
6. **Be great at setting the client's expectations**. As I point out in chapter 13, I never overcommitted without regret. Setting the client's expectations early in the sales process will yield rewards when it's time to negotiate a contract.
7. **Be creative**. This comes naturally to a few people; however, it can be a learned skill. As you develop experience with selling, keep track of what works and what doesn't. The dynamics of selling are ever-changing, and the successful salesperson learns quickly to adapt to these changes.
8. **Be focused**. Sell only the things you can deliver. Listen very carefully to the prospective client's reasons for going out to bid; these will identify hot buttons that will greatly inform your RFP responses and your software demonstrations.

9. **Be a team leader**. The good salesperson understands the huge team it takes to sell to a client. It is the salesperson's role to be the quarterback of the team, tracking every team event as if success depends upon it; it does.
10. **Be a detective**. Years ago a popular television show featured Peter Falk as Columbo. He was a bumbling detective seemingly out of touch with the key parts of the murder case under investigation. He asked all kinds of questions, but in the end, all those questions led him to the unlikely guilty party. His unassuming and genuine way of asking questions caught people off guard, and they found themselves revealing more than they intended.

The successful salesperson in a complex software system sale learns everything about the prospect from every angle. There is no need for pretense or an overblown sense of self-importance, just a genuine interest in truly understanding the prospective client from every angle. The more you can learn, the better you can present your product in the light that makes it a clear and honest match for what the customer really needs. If in the process you discover that your product is not that match, stop wasting time and move on.

## Buying Influences and the Coach

Drake identifies the three categories of buyers and explains the critical role of a coach. When you read the RFP, you get a sense for the type of buyer with whom you are dealing. The first buyer type is the **user**. This means that the users in the various departments will have the most significant role in the choice of a vendor. For these user buyers, you must carefully prepare and execute your software demonstration after you have crafted your RFP responses to the end users.

The second buyer type is the **technical** buyer. In these cases, it is likely that the IT department will select the next vendor. Your RFP responses must be formulated (or, at least, edited) by your technical staff. A few phone calls to the folks in IT will help guide you in your responses. Then, when it's time to do the demo, you better have the presenter be up to speed on the technical side. In qualifying the technical buyer, find out if he or she has a preferred hardware platform and database management system; if he or she does and you don't support it, walk away from the deal—you're not going to win.

The third buyer type is the **economic** buyer. The price components of a proposal consist of the software license fee, annual support fees, professional services for the implementation, cost of third-party software, annual support on third-party software, hardware, and travel costs. Try to determine the overall budget for the prospective client; then, be realistic in your evaluation of the competition. It makes no sense to chase a deal where the prospect simply can't afford your solution.

Drake tells the students what a vital role is played by a **coach**. The coach is someone in the prospect's organization who is rooting for you to win. This may be someone with whom you have previously worked, or someone who used your software at another institution. Coaches can give you invaluable advice on how to win the deal. They can identify the decision makers, the buyer types, and the hot buttons for selection. Typically, they have firsthand knowledge of the aspects of the current system that the users do not like.

***Lesson: Try to find a coach.***

## Contract Elements

The elements of a software sales contract typically include the following:

1. **Software grant and use restrictions**. This is where you limit the use of the package to the institution making the purchase.
2. **Warranty**. In this section, the contract will make it clear that expectations about the performance of the software are strictly limited to what the documentation says the software will do and nothing more. This area is getting more complex all the time, and attorneys spend a lot of time arguing over the finer points. Sometimes, when there is a functional software checklist

involved in the purchase process, you also have to warrant that the software will do what is in the checklist. If you decide to agree to that request, you should go through the checklist again carefully and clarify any answers you gave at the courting stage to make sure the understanding that is provided is complete enough to be relied upon as contractual.

3. **Indemnifications**. This is where you hold the parties harmless in special events, such as acts of God.
4. **Limitation on liability**. This is where you clearly state that your company is not liable if someone uses your software to write himself or herself a million-dollar check.
5. **Special provisions**. The most common special provisions are related to the scope of work. An example might be that certain performances related to a project implementation plan or planned customizations might be included. These will only be needed when your company is performing substantial professional services in conjunction with the use of the software.
6. **Product and services price schedule**. Make sure you allow for uplifts in future years, typically based upon the CPI.
7. **Payment terms**. This can be different with each contract; try to get the client to adopt your standard contract. Payment may be based upon certain milestones, such as going live on the general ledger; or upon percent of completion as it relates to the implementation project. Because this has a dramatic impact upon your ability to recognize revenue, be careful in drawing up the payment terms.
8. **Annual support schedule**. This is where you lay out the annual support fees—really important to a company that wants to be acquired because it represents recurrent revenue. Recurrent revenue gives a higher multiple in the acquisition price.
9. **Escrow agreement**. The provision for an escrow agreement is provided to assure the buyer that if you go out of business, they can still have authorized access to the software and also be allowed to get the source code so they can support it themselves. This provision is commonly insisted upon in large complex deals.

> The reality is that with software products as they are today, the complexity and many third-party elements of many software systems make it pretty impractical for any end-user customer to actually support the software themselves.

The most astute buyers will know this, and the less-informed ones will insist on the provision even after you explain that they probably can't support the software themselves anyway. For this reason, just establish a relationship with an escrow company, place your software in escrow with them, and include escrow provisions in your standard contract. The fees to the escrow company for release to the end user should be paid by the end-user entity. This makes sense because in the event of an actual dissolution of the company, they want their relationship to be direct with the escrow company, which can release the code to them directly.

## Contract Negotiation

So, you've gone through all the persuasive points and buying criteria, including demonstrating that it is the desired solution, showing your company's financial strength, showing the track record of success, and selling the hardware platform. You've provided client references and disclosed pricing, and the prospect has picked your company. Drake lays out these important factors when negotiating a software sales contract.

1. Sell the terms from the start. Once a prospect is identified as *in* the funnel, let him or her know what the terms are for your standard contract. This is also an important data point in disqualifying a prospect—that is, if their terms are way out of line, walk away from the deal.
2. Try very hard to have your standard-form contract be the instrument upon which the negotiation is to be based. This is not always possible, particularly with very large, highly visible clients. Clients like Salt Lake City and Harris County, Texas, had their own, somewhat onerous, form contracts.

3. Have them review the standard-form contact; then, assess the gap between your standard terms and the ones the prospect is proposing.
4. Face-to-face meetings are best; however, many contracts are negotiated in lengthy conference calls. Make sure you know who the prospect expects to be involved in the negotiations—generally the marketing and sales VP, sometimes the president.
5. Use silence. When negotiating, a good strategy is to make your point, even when you think they may not agree, and then just wait for them to respond. You will be tempted to rush in and fill the silence with your next-best proposal. Don't. Just wait to see how they respond. You may be surprised that your first proposal may be acceptable after all.
6. Use a parking lot. When you run into sticky items that you just can't initially agree on, put them in a parking lot and move on to other items. This way the client will know that you still have to work through these hard items, but it is a lot easier to decide if you can be flexible on some things after you have fewer open issues.
7. If you give up a provision, try to get something in trade. Drake was a master at this. This is why he urges you to understand the entire list of terms and conditions before you yield on any of them.

***Lesson: It does you no good to horse-trade if you're out of horses.***

8. Involve your decision makers up front. Before you start negotiations, you should know who the parties are that will be making the final decisions for the prospective client. Try to get those final decision makers to be part of the negotiations from the start.

## Drake's Sales and Marketing Division

A marketing division can be formulated in many ways. Drake's division matured, and the company experienced dramatic growth. Drake shows the students how he put together his team. He first listed the organizational questions that led him to the adopted structure. He considered an internal sales force or distributors. Then, he considered territories: size, vertical or horizontal representation, geographic divisions, time zones, matching quota with opportunity, and territory and channel conflicts. Demo support was a key factor in his organization, as was his belief in the value of a presales staff.

First, he appointed one marketing manager and one staff member. Second, he created a demo-support team, consisting of two people for the financial suite, two people for the personnel suite, and one person to manage the demo systems. Third, Drake divided his sales force into two people for higher education, two for our K–12 vertical market, two for the governmental market, and three to represent our installed base of clients. Fourth, he appointed two people in administrative sales support responsible for proposal generation. Finally, he appointed two people for presales support; their job was prospecting. That's a total of twenty-one full-time employees, including Drake, to generate sales. Every one of those employees was critical to the success and continued growth of the company.

Drake completed this class unit by listing the necessary sales resources used at Bi-Tech: prospect lists, CRM system, price template, proposal template, data sheets, success stories, and travel budget.

## Important Stories

Drake concluded his fast-paced second lecture by sharing some important stories, each with a message. I asked Drake to add the text for each of these stories. These are Drake's words.

1. **Twenty-Dollar Wedding**: A comic strip from years gone by (*Li'l Abner*) featured a small-town preacher who offered to perform weddings for various fees. The standard wedding was five dollars, with traditional but brief citations from the Bible ending with "I do" from both parties. For ten dollars, the couple could write their own vows, and the preacher would incorporate those into

the ceremony. If they wanted the church decorated special, then fifteen bucks. The top-of-the-line wedding in this hillbilly town was a ceremony featuring all of the above and culminating with the preacher putting on a show: wrestling a live alligator at some point in the celebration for entertainment. This wedding was big, and no effort or expense was spared.

***Lesson: With some of your demonstrations, you need to pull out all the stops.***

Stun the prospect with a demonstration that is truly unexpected. Convert some of their data. Create their favorite report just for the demo. Use examples from their most stubborn challenges in their existing software. This is a level of effort you can't do every time, but with the projects that are "must-win," really shock the prospect with your attention to detail, and you will be the victor.

2. **How Many Toppings**: A startup company needs to be run on a budget. Every person who spends money in the business should feel the urgency to use the resources of the business as if the money were their own. Gary Sitton had a way of letting every employee feel the weight of being frugal with the limited company resources. One day in the very early days of Bi-Tech, we had the chance to do a joint prospecting effort with IBM to attract joint customers. It was agreed that IBM would send two representatives from their Sacramento office to Chico to work with the Bi-Tech sales team for a whole day doing phone prospecting. As a show of gratitude for their travel, we agreed to cover the cost of lunch for the group. Because Bi-Tech was so very careful with every dime, it was pretty unusual to buy lunch for anyone at that point in the growth of the business.

   The day was successful, and when the IBMers left for the day, Gary came by to get a report. We told him of our successful efforts and about the pizza lunch we provided. Since this was outside of the normal operating approach at the time, there was a feeling that maybe we should have asked Gary's blessing before buying lunch. When we told him about the pizza lunch we provided, we tried to read his expression; was that too extravagant? Gary's first comment upon learning of the pizza lunch seemed tense: "How many toppings?" With a little trepidation that maybe we had gone too far, we searched his eyes. A twinkle soon arrived, revealing that he was toying with us.

***Lesson: Being careful with even small expenditures is important in a startup business.***

3. **Everybody Has Dirty Socks**: Formal procurement processes are often done by using a written and detailed Request for Proposal. These documents are sometimes overwhelming. They can be hundreds of pages long, with everything from contractual demands to detailed specifications for every item. In about 1994, we responded to one of these really detailed RFPs. This one had a requirement that the winning vendor include a performance bond. This is basically an insurance policy for the client that if the vendor fails, there will be money provided by the bond company to complete the project anyway. With these kinds of performance bonds, the payment for the bond premium is paid by the vendor.

   After the bid was sent in, to my great horror, I realized that we had not priced the deal to include the expense of the bond. I was so frustrated that I had missed this point. In the end it would not be fatal, and even with this mistake, the margin on the deal would allow a good profit, but missing something like that is unacceptable. When I realized the mistake, I went to Gary's office and just fessed up. I told him of the error, and I told him my plan was that it would never happen again. No excuse, just a statement of what happened, what I learned, and how I would ensure this would never happen again. As a manager myself, I never expected that an employee's performance would always be flawless, but if an employee learned from each mistake and took responsibility for it, I was always pleased. Employees who wanted to spend their time and mine telling me why it was not their fault could work somewhere else.

Excuses are a lot like dirty socks; we all have them, and they all stink. If you want to be a top employee or a top sales and marketing contributor, don't make excuses. Just learn from the mistake, acknowledge it, resolve that it won't be repeated, and move on. Everyone who is trying new things to succeed will make a mistake now and then. The trick is to make sure your mistakes are small and infrequent and that you learn from every one of them.

***Lesson: Don't spend any energy making excuses when you goof.***

4. **Thank-You Cards and Letters Home**: The power of a thank-you note cannot be overestimated. Earlier in the book it was noted that Judy Sitton was consistently sent to meet with upset clients and resolve their concerns. One of the reasons Judy was so successful at this was because of her genuine connection to the people. Whether clients or employees, one of the methods that Judy employed was to write a personal note. When you get a personal note from someone these days in his or her own handwriting with a stamp on it, that is rare. And when the note acknowledges you as a human being, not just a business contact, that is even more rare; and when it comes with a dose of humanity and warmth like the ones Judy always sent, you just feel good.

   One day in 1994, my parents came to visit from Utah. When they arrived they were excited to show me a letter they had received from Gary Sitton. I could not imagine why Gary would write my parents a letter. How did he even get their address? In the letter Gary just told my parents how he felt about working with me. It was not hollow flattery; it was just genuine appreciation.

   With this one letter, Gary captured my loyalty even more

fully. The letter was the most heartfelt and honest expression of admiration for me that I had ever read. It made my parents so proud. It made me feel so important. It made me feel that I'd never want to let this man down. Gary was just doing what he and Judy often did. There was no ulterior motive, just a way of letting me know that I was a valued employee. As a business owner, if you can let your employees feel like Gary and Judy made me feel, they will give you much more than their hours of labor. They will give their loyalty and their hearts.

***Lesson: Shower employees with caring and make them feel part of the family.***

5. **Christmas and Birthday Gifts**: When Judy called and asked if she could take our five children Christmas shopping, I could not believe it. After a demanding day at the office, she still had time for this? She did! Treating employees' families with care will surprise them and will make them feel that they are all part of something much more important than just a company that provides a paycheck. Employees with this level of caring from the people they work for will feel that their work is much more important than the compensation that is provided. That will cause them to want to contribute at a higher level than could ever be expected from a salary or wage earner.

***Lesson: Treating your employees with kindness is always a great investment.***

6. **Yes, That Is Your Paycheck**: When you find an employee who is willing to give you more than you expected, then surprise that employee by giving him or her something unexpected! In 1993 my paycheck was delivered to my desk by the internal delivery person. I was busy when it arrived, but before the day ended, I opened it to see if any commissions were included. I could not believe my eyes. The check was written for many hundreds of

dollars more than I was expecting. I searched the pay advice for any explanation of why the amount was so large. I could not find any reason for the large amount. I puzzled over seeing Gary's signature and thinking how unlike Gary it was to make a large mistake like this with so much money.

After some thought, I walked across the building to Gary's office and told him that my paycheck had an error; I was paid way more than I was due. Gary did not even look at the check to consider the error. He just said matter-of-factly, "There is no mistake. You are worth every penny we are paying you and more, so we put more in your paycheck this time to acknowledge that. You have earned it. Any other questions?"

My mouth hung open with awe. I had never been treated this way. I was shocked. I certainly had no more questions, and as I walked back to my desk, I was on cloud nine. Being treated like that made me want to walk through brick walls for this man.

***Lesson: Surprise your employees now and then (when they deserve it) and see what they will do for you.***

7. **We Don't Know If We Can Handle Six Hundred Users**: Be brutally honest, and your customers will trust you. In 1993, when we sold the city of Salt Lake, they insisted they would need six hundred concurrent users. I was in one of the finalizing meetings where this demand was placed on Bi-Tech. I knew we did not have any customers anywhere near that large. I knew that the software had never been tested at that level. It was not my place to say what we could or could not do; the question was being directed to Gary.

   Before he spoke, I was thinking of an optimistic statement that would give the customer assurance. I was not sure what Gary was thinking until he said to Bill Haight (Salt Lake's CIO), "I don't know if the software will handle that many users, Bill." I was expecting Bill to run from the room, screaming. Instead, a very productive and realistic plan for proving what the software would do was devised. Trust was high.

***Lesson: Blunt honesty gives rise to a partnership.***

Gary agreed to provisions that would protect Salt Lake if we could not do it, and Bill agreed to participate in the testing processes that would be run. In the end, the relationship was made stronger as the parties worked together, rather than the traditional dance of the vendor promising whatever would be expedient to get the deal and then trying later to see if they can actually deliver.

That concludes the Drake Brown chapter. Believe me, the students got their money's worth in the two 110-minute presentations. Drake is one of the most honorable and hardworking professionals I have come to know in my career. Great employee, great friend, great father, great husband, and great man!

# 3

## Human Resources: Took Calculus for Fun

Kristi Bennett

Back in the eighties, we were starting to grow and needed to hire someone to work on documentation. James Bennett suggested we interview his girlfriend, Kristi. Asked what her major was, he responded, "Home economics." While this major focuses on clothing, textiles, nutrition, and other important disciplines, I wondered how it would translate to a software company. As said previously, a college transcript was required to interview for a position.

When Kristi came to the interview, a review of her transcripts showed she had taken calculus. When I asked her why she took calculus, she quipped, "Just for fun." She was hired on the spot.

Once Kristi was hired, we quickly began to explore her other talents. Of our employee base, Kristi worked in the most departments: marketing, sales, tech support, product management, consulting, documentation, and even being the 5:00 a.m. voice for our East Coast clients. Kristi came to know "human resources" through writing the HR user manual; knowing the system well enough to write the guide, she became a consultant to clients implementing the software. Probably her most memorable experience was at Stanford University in 1989, when the Loma Prieta earthquake struck. Kristi was preparing for a session in a building on campus that was heavily damaged and then stranded at a local hotel until the next day, when I sent the company plane to pick her up.

When Kristi was promoted to vice president of HR, she was given two directives: "Don't tell me anything personal about the employees and keep me out of jail." Of course, Kristi would not have violated an employee's privacy, but I wanted it to be clear that my business decisions are based on employee merit and business needs. HR, more than any other part of a business, is the most onerous in terms of rules and regulations. Failing to follow these rules and regulations can put an end to your company. Kristi kept me out of jail and ensured that Bi-Tech was compliant with the myriad requirements of HR.

Kristi and James were married in 1986 and raised two fine sons, Zachary and Taylor. James and Kristi became godparents to our two children. Kristi's illustrious career is a testament to her brilliance, attention to detail, and common sense.

Kristi has over twenty years as an HR professional. After Bi-Tech was acquired, she continued working in human resources, holding various roles, including the lead global HR business partner at the president and division CEO level, managing global HR operations/systems and the global HR budget process/review.

Kristi has managed benefit plans and incentive compensation, provided due-diligence research for acquisitions, managed mad employees and supervisors, ensured that payroll was timely and accurate, and dealt with state and federal audits and a variety of other tasks required to keep employees happy, the company out of hot water, and the boss out of jail. Kristi's lecture was fast-paced and extremely well-organized; no surprise there. On a personal note, Kristi has the distinction of having the messiest office of any employee ever hired. Papers and files stacked twelve inches high cover her entire desk. I used to give her hell about it. The amazing part was, if you asked her where something was, she could find it in seconds. I'll bet her office is still a terrible mess! Most of what follows was taken directly from Kristi's PowerPoint slides.

## What Is Human Resources?

Kristi opens with, "Let's be clear about the role of human resources; we are not the party planners of the company! While we may have great ideas just like the other departments, this is not our specialty. I won't say we don't get involved with parties, but it is on a different level than you may think." Imagine the challenges a company may face when there is alcohol served at a company function and employees behave poorly, or the Halloween event, a family affair, finds participants inappropriately costumed. What is the real role of the HR professional? Human resource professionals have a role in the company helping manage one of the largest expenses a company has, its labor force. The labor that comes from that expense is what can help you be profitable. To run an effective business, you must ensure that every dollar is spent wisely, and that includes the huge investment in your employees.

Kristi cautions the students that she can't possibly cover everything about HR in less than two hours. She recommends an excellent website and encourages the students to visit http://www.dir.ca.gov/dlse/; and if they stop by my office, they can refer to the *California Labor Law Digest* that she loaned me for the semester. It is amusing that they call it a digest. It is over two inches thick, 979 8½ x 11–inch pages, in small print. That's just for California. The federal government has a similar site, http://www.dol.gov/compliance. Each state has its own regulations, and compliance with those regulations is a must when employees fall under those jurisdictions. Being familiar with the requirements is essential.

Kristi also encourages those in the class who are employed to read the legally required posters that should be posted in their workplace where employees have regular and reasonable access (typically break rooms). Most states have their own set of employment regulations (as do some cities and counties); typically whatever is most advantageous to the employee is the one that rules. Keeping track of the myriad of regulations where you have employees located is a necessity.

Human resources is about managing your human capital, maintaining compliance with federal, state, and local law, and strategizing with the business. In managing your human capital, you must recruit and retain the best employees. You also want to link people strategy with the strategy of the business. In other words, find the best fit.

Most employers try to perform the HR functions on their own, until they reach a critical mass where the employee issues are becoming a distraction to running the business or there is a violation and the business needs help. There are two main categories of HR professionals, generalist and specialist. When a company is beginning to grow, it typically hires an HR generalist. Then, as the company becomes much larger, one or more HR specialists may be hired to address particular areas. Examples of some HR specialist functions are:

- business partner
- recruiting
- training and learning development
- compensation
- benefits
- employee relations
- operations, including service center and payroll
- risk management, particularly in health and safety

## Important Classifications

Kristi introduces the students to some very important classifications for people who work for your company. First, she explains the difference between an employee and an independent contractor (IC). Second, she highlights the difference between exempt and nonexempt employees.

When you hire an employee, you are obligated to withhold and remit statutory taxes. These include FIT, SIT, SS, Medicare, and other deductions mandated by state and local statute. You, as an employer, are also required to obtain and pay for Workers Compensation. With an IC, you have no Workers Compensation obligation. While this may sound good, you can still be held liable for an injury incurred while on your property. ICs have no employment tax deductions, have no rights to employee benefits, are not covered by state and federal wage and hour laws, and are not entitled to unemployment insurance benefits from your account.

Before hiring someone as an IC, you should fully understand the work relationship and ask yourself many questions before determining the IC status. Multiple state and federal agencies apply different tests to determine if an IC is actually an employee. Kristi advises the students to follow the most stringent tests. The following are among the many questions that help determine if the person is properly classified as an IC.

- Do you supervise or instruct the IC? ICs are free to do the job in their own way, however they want.
- Can the IC quit or be fired at any time? ICs are engaged to perform a job and cannot be fired before the job is complete, unless the terms of the contract are violated.

***Lesson: Be specific in your contract with independent contractors.***

- Is the IC doing work that others in your employ are doing? If so, he or she is likely not an IC.
- Does the IC have a separately established business? Does the IC hold himself or herself out to the general public for work? If not, he or she is likely not an IC.
- Do you furnish tools, equipment, and supplies? If so, again likely not an IC.
- Can the IC make business decisions that impact his or her profitability? In other words, does the IC control his or her equipment, facilities, and intellectual property? If not, he or she probably is not an IC.
- Does the IC have a substantial investment that would subject him or her to financial risk and possible loss? If not, again probably not an IC.
- Is the work unskilled or semiskilled labor? If so, probably not an IC.
- Is the IC being paid a fixed salary, hourly wage, or piece rate? ICs typically get paid for the job and are paid upon completion of projects.
- Did the worker previously perform the same or similar service for you as an employee? If so, probably not an IC.
- Does the IC believe he or she is an employee? If so, not an IC.

Kristi clearly laid out the consequences of misclassification of an IC. Employment taxes and penalties must be paid from the date the IC was hired. Back wage and hour requirements will be applied, as well as compensation for benefits missed. Willful misclassification includes civil penalties for violation. Thousands of dollars can be levied for each violation, in addition to other sanctions.

***Lesson: Know what classifies a worker as an independent contractor.***

Kristi's next unit deals with the classification of an employee as exempt or nonexempt. These are very important classifications, and as with ICs, they carry very costly penalties if they are improperly followed. Exempt employees have wage requirements, and they are not entitled to receive pay for overtime work. Exempt-employee classifications generally include executives (typically managerial), administrative, professional, computer professional, commissioned outside salespeople, and others. Nonexempt employees are those who do not meet one or more of the exemptions, and they have required meal and rest periods and must be paid at least minimum wage, and their hours and days of work are regulated, at least in California (other states may differ).

***Lesson: When in doubt, classify as nonexempt.***

Exempt employees must pass these duty tests.

- Must have discretion and independent judgment, customarily and regularly. This means frequently, in the course of day-to-day activities, they are not following prescribed procedures from memory.
- Must have the power to make independent choices pertaining to matters of significance, and be free from immediate supervision that pertains to the business or customers.

- Must have the ability to make a recommendation for action that can be subject to a superior's final authority. The employee must possess sufficient authority of the recommendations to affect matters of consequence to the business or customers.
- Examples of exempt duties include advising management, planning, negotiating, representing the company, procurement, analyzing and researching, and determining company and personnel policies. Other exempt duties include interviewing, selecting, and training employees; setting, adjusting, and recommending pay and work hours; directing work; handling employee complaints; disciplining employees; distributing work; and evaluating employee efficiency.
- The wage test for administrative employees in California, subject to change, is two times the annual minimum wage, $33,280 to $37,440. The same test is applied to the executive exemption and to the professional exemption. The current wage test for a computer professional is $83,132 to $84,130.
- The wage test for a computer professional was much higher in 2007, $103,522. To pass the wage test, be prepared to "chase the wage," as the rate of increase can exceed what your budget may allow. Computer professionals must be engaged primarily in intellectual and creative work, exercising discretion and independent judgment. They must be highly skilled and proficient in systems-analysis techniques, consulting with users to determine hardware and software system functional specifications. They are involved in designing, developing, documenting, analyzing, creating, testing, or modifying computer systems and programs related to user or system design specifications.
- The outside sales exemption requires eighteen-plus years of age, 50 percent or more working away from the place of business, and 50 percent or more of the duties can't be incidental to other duties, like delivering goods.

The job title does not matter. Exempt employee misclassification is highly litigated. Bad things happen if you misclassify exempt employees:

retroactive overtime payments, missed meal and rest break pay, waiting-time penalties, and attorney fees, to name a few.

***Lesson: Inaccurate exempt classification can cost your company money.***

Special protections apply to nonexempt employees in California and other states. They get a ten-minute rest period for every four hours, unless three and a half hours completes the shift. A thirty-minute meal period for every five hours worked must be provided, unless the shift ends in six hours. Both the employee and employer must agree to waive the meal period in writing. The company owes one hour of pay for each meal period missed. Kristi asserts that many employees feel that to be classified as nonexempt is a reduction in stature. That is not the case; it's a matter of employment law.

Kristi also tells the students the company must keep impeccable records on nonexempt employees. In California, overtime pay kicks in when the employee works more than eight hours in a day, more than forty hours in a week, and seven consecutive days in a workweek. Reporting time pay applies to the employee being called to work and then sent home, or called to work twice in one day.

***Lesson: Keep accurate records of nonexempt employees.***

## The Hiring Process

Kristi divides the hiring process into five parts: posting the job, the interview, reference checks, the offer, and bringing the employee onboard. For posting the job, be extremely clear about the job duties and requirements, indicating level of education, years of experience, and any other factors that can be objectively measured. Avoid statements like, "Repairman (implies male), perfect for a single person willing to travel (marital status), waitress (implies female), and young and energetic (age discrimination)."

Great caution must be displayed during the interview. Select resumes that meet the requirements. Conduct consistent interviews. Ask only job-related, nondiscriminatory questions. Educate anyone who will interview the candidate. Assess the candidate after the interview with clear notes: for example, "not impressed" is weak; "does not have experience with necessary equipment" is solid. Interview more than once if the first interview went well. Get references and check them all.

***Lesson: Interview standards can help avoid litigation.***

Kristi completes the unit on interviews by listing bad and good questions for the interview. Bad questions are:

- What year did you graduate from university? You may ask what university he or she attended.
- Are you a US citizen? You may ask, "If you are hired, can you provide evidence that you are legally able to work inside the United States?" You must ask this of all applicants if it's asked of any.
- Do you have children? You can ask if overtime work is acceptable.

Good questions are:

- Are you willing and able to travel (if the job requires travel)?
- Why did you apply for this job?
- What do you consider the greatest accomplishment in your career?
- Why are you leaving your current job?
- What type of environment do you prefer, individual or team?
- What qualifications do you possess for this job?
- How has your prior experience helped you to prepare for this job?

When it comes time to make the formal offer, make sure you include each of the following:

- Offer should be in writing.
- Job title.
- Exempt/nonexempt status.
- Compensation and the basis: salary or hourly or piece rate.
- Regular payday.
- Legal name of the employer, DBA.
- Work address and mailing address.
- Employer's phone number.
- Full- or part-time classification for benefits.
- Workers Compensation details.
- Official hire date.
- Statement of at-will employment—that is, either party may terminate for any reason.
- Deadline to transact signed offer of acceptance.
- Conditions to which the offer is subject, for example, drug testing, background checking, medical examinations.
- Noncompeting requirements, if they apply.

***Lesson: The formal job offer must clearly state many details.***

Kristi moves on to the important aspects of bringing the new employee onboard. Have the workstation ready on his or her first day. Make sure that team members know the new hire is starting. Introduce the new employee to colleagues. Set the employee's expectations; give direction. Get the new hire engaged; he or she is costing you money now.

Day-one paperwork includes the following:

- Form I-9. This is the employment eligibility verification.
- Rights to Workers Compensation benefits. Include the personal physician designation form and the personal chiropractor/acupuncturist designation form.
- State disability insurance provisions.
- Paid family-leave pamphlet.
- Notice of COBRA continuation coverage.

- Sexual-harassment pamphlet.
- W-4 wage withholding allowance certificate; DE4 if he or she requests it.
- Permit to employ and work; this is for minors.
- Wage and employment notice.

Day-one training should include:

- Safety training, for example, fire exits, extinguishers, emergency evacuation meeting location.
- Workstation evaluation, checking ergonomics.
- Policies and work rules.
- Benefits availability and eligibility; sign up.
- Confidentiality expectations.
- Sexual-harassment training.
- Internet, e-mail, and cell phone usage policies.
- Receipt of employee handbook.
- Sign-off on employer property and equipment.

***Lesson: The first day on the job should be well planned and informed.***

Kristi also lists important office postings that should be included in a common area, for example, the break room. Other postings may be required depending on the nature of the business.

- Industrial Welfare Commission Wage Order
- Payday notice
- Emergency phone numbers
- No-smoking signage
- Workers Compensation benefits
- Log of occupational injuries and illnesses
- Pregnancy disability (5–49 employees in California)
- Notice to employees on unemployment, disability, and family leave

- Equal employment opportunity
- Polygraph Protection Act
- Minimum wage
- Safety and health protection
- Whistleblower protection
- Time off to vote
- Workers Compensation carrier and coverage
- Discrimination and harassment in employment prohibited
- Family care and medical leave and pregnancy disability leave (fifty-plus employees in California)
- Notice to employee for unemployment insurance benefits
- FMLA (Family Medical Leave Act)

***Lesson: Make sure your employee postings are complete; it is the law.***

This critical segment of her unit on hiring culminates in some sage advice. Get employee sign-off on all paperwork issued and received. Obtain employee and employer sign-off on all training delivered. Provide a copy of sign-offs to the employee, with the originals in the employee's file.

***Lesson: A paper trail can save you.***

## Employee Relations

Here, Kristi takes the students through employee complaints, performance reviews, and terminations. Employee complaints can run the gambit from "My coworker has body odor" to "My boss keeps asking me to have drinks on Saturday night at his place to go over my work performance." Kristi encourages students to use their common sense in dealing with each issue. If a labor law is being violated, take swift and decisive action. If no law is being broken, attempt to mitigate the issue with one-on-one discussions.

***Lesson: Personnel issues require common sense.***

Performance reviews are important because they let employees know how they are meeting, or failing to meet, expectations. Remember, you are investing in the employee to perform a job. If that job is not being done, your investment is being wasted. As an employer, you should set goals and have good metrics by which to measure the achievement of these goals. Your employee should never be left to wonder if he or she is performing to the company's expectations. Regular performance reviews should be conducted to ensure that the employee is working on the right goals and performing duties at the expected level. Where employees are underperforming, they need to know sooner, rather than later, to make corrections. Never wait for the next evaluation period to make a necessary midcourse correction. Of course, if the employee is performing well, he or she should regularly be informed of this also. Document the performance meetings, especially if there is a performance problem. At least once a year, a formal written evaluation should be conducted (with quarterly or semiannual status checks). An employee should never be surprised during an annual review; regular meetings will help ensure this.

Terminating an employee is the one role that nobody enjoys. Terminations are typically due to business downsizing (lack of work/lack of funds) or poor performance. Where the business is downsizing, a careful evaluation should be made of the positions no longer required. When selecting the positions to be eliminated, care must be taken to ensure that the selection process is not made in violation of any law (e.g., age of incumbent). When making a performance-based termination, consider the performance evaluations, corrective action, any policy violations, and so on. In any case, for an involuntary termination, the employee is due all wages through the termination date, including any accrued balance for vacation or floating holiday (in California). Ensure that the employee is provided required unemployment insurance paperwork. Be prepared to respond to any claim for unemployment benefits by the terminated employee. If you dispute the claim, additional information will be required to justify why you don't believe the former worker is due unemployment benefits. Oftentimes, an unemployment hearing will be held; in these cases you will want all facts and written documentation with you when addressing the judge.

***Lesson: Keep good documentation and make fair employment decisions.***

In closing, being an employer of choice in the community is a big plus. How you treat your employees will set the company's reputation and be a driver for getting good talent to help your business grow. What your employees say about working for their supervisor and the company, including their coworkers, is great advertising (which can be good or bad, and you want it to be good). Treat your employees fairly and reward them for their contribution (verbally, a token gift card to their favorite restaurant, or a spot bonus). Kristi pointed out in her presentation the many ways that Judy and Gary were successful in Bi-Tech as an employer of choice. One example noted described the handwritten notes given to employees pointing out specifics on a job well-done. This made it clear to employees that management is aware. Often these notes included spot bonuses or gift cards to favorite vendors for even greater impact. The personal touch goes a long way to enhancing employee engagement.

Kristi certainly hit the critical high points to help the students understand the pivotal and demanding role played by HR. I wish she had time to give one more lecture. She has considerable knowledge of outsourcing people and tasks, co-location vs. multiple offices, working from home, due diligence for acquisitions, compensation outside the base, commission plans, and cultural absorption issues when companies combine. Actually, Kristi could do an entire semester on HR if she weren't flying all over the world.

# 4

## Customer Service and Employee Recognition: Amazing Grace

Judy Sitton

The company began in Judy's dining room. Her husband, Gary, developed the first version of the software in the late seventies, and as demand grew, began to hire some of his best students as the first employees of Bi-Tech. Gary taught computer science at CSU, Chico, for seventeen-plus years, resigning his full professorship in the early eighties.

For the first eight years, the company was run out of our home, an A-frame located in the foothills of the Sierra Nevada Mountains, at three thousand feet elevation, approximately twenty-five minutes from Chico. In the first few years, Judy was still teaching fourth grade and was quite busy with being mother to Holly and Mark, both still in grammar school. She still found time to make waffles for any employee who showed up to work early or was still there after pulling an all-nighter. And after a full day of teaching, she would come home and help with the office duties of the growing company.

The early years could best be described as "chaotic industry." As the company added employees, Judy cut back to part-time teaching so that she could assume more of the administrative demands of a growing company. Without one word of complaint, she endured three major remodels of the A-frame to convert it into a nine-thousand-square-foot business/home. She spent one winter remodel with a sheet of plastic separating the bedroom from the snow on the ground outside. When she reached a point where she was making waffles for seventeen employees, the decision was made to move to a "real" office building.

In 1983, Judy assumed full-time responsibilities at Bi-Tech. Her initial duties involved general office management (A/R, A/P, payroll, and client management); however, as the software package became more complex and the client base grew, an office manager was hired, and Judy took on the role of training clients in the use of the software. Training clients on a complex highly integrated (and somewhat brittle) software package takes a very special set of skills. Judy's approach was "If I can teach fourth-graders to read, write, and do arithmetic, I can teach adults to use a software package that has bugs." It is this positive "can do, no matter what" attitude that made Judy such a successful businesswoman. In her free time, flying to and from a client site, Judy would develop training aids and documentation. The clients that were trained by Judy still say she was the best software "teacher" they ever had.

As the company continued to grow, Judy took on the role of training the trainers; then, when the employee count passed fifty, she became the executive vice president. In this role, she performed many demanding duties. Beyond dealing with a president (Gary) who thought people should just know how to use software, perhaps Judy's most demanding role involved working with "clients in crisis." When an implementation was going badly or a client had significant key personnel changes, Judy was the one who would get the client back on track. With site visits, Gantt charts that would fill a large wall, and weekly, often daily, conference calls, Judy would work each problem through to resolution. Judy's attention to detail and preparedness are legendary in the industry. As her husband puts it, "She grinds it up into a fine dust."

Judy was keenly aware of the R & D demands and heavy delivery schedules that attend a growing software company. However, she always took on the role of client advocate, making sure that everyone in the company knew that clients should be treated as Bi-Tech's employees would expect to be treated by a vendor. It is not Judy's nature to be dogmatic and assertive; but rather, to rely on an employee's common sense, energy, and caring to dictate how problems are addressed. She is also blessed with that intangible character trait that makes people not want to disappoint her.

**_Lesson: It's important that your employees act as client advocates._**

As Bi-Tech grew to well over a hundred employees, Judy's role became even more important. She continued to work with clients in crisis, but she also helped form the management infrastructure of Bi-Tech. As vice presidents began to be added for R & D, human resources, training, marketing, client services, finance, and quality assurance, Judy provided the invaluable "character instinct" to advise who could (and could not) do the job.

In addition to her many roles as executive vice president, Judy was also responsible for coordinating one national and two regional user group meetings each year. Many software companies find that user group meetings are a colossal gripe session to be endured; not Bi-Tech. Judy would prepare for each meeting as if it were the only thing she had to do. Not only was she able to remember the name and face of every attendee, but she often knew the names of their kids. Every session was well planned, organized, and delivered—no average feat when you have over five hundred people attending a user conference. Judy did not make friends with these people because they were clients; she made friends with them because they were people.

Even as the company grew to over two hundred employees and over three hundred clients, Judy continued to handle the biggest clients in crisis. Perhaps this falls under the category of "no good deed goes unpunished," but Judy was, hands down, the best person to change an unhappy client into one you want on your client reference list.

Simply put, Judy was the conscience of Bi-Tech. She never operates from a personal agenda or a self-centered ego. She asks hard questions that people don't always want to hear. She exhibits a work ethic that defines "lead by example." The genuine caring and love she has for employees and clients can't be faked. She allows her husband to be the head of the family and the business, understanding full well that she is the neck and can turn that head anywhere she wants (from *My Big Fat Greek Wedding*).

Writing this introduction as her husband, I must say Judy is, without a doubt, the toughest person I know. She has been a type 1 diabetic since she was twenty-five. She has taken up to five insulin shots a day, with twice that many blood tests, and has never, in all these years, complained once about having the disease or shown one moment of self-pity. During those years when I was nonstop on the road selling and developing software, she ran a multimillion-dollar company and never once asked for more help or griped about the stress. She has dealt with the worst personal tragedy, the death of our son, yet continues to focus her caring on others. After forty-seven years of being married to Judy, I consider myself quite fortunate to have a spouse that often says, "I am so happy to be alive." That sort of thing rubs off on you.

Judy continues her community work. She served eleven years on the Enloe Medical Center Board, many of those as vice chair. She has served many years as president of the Gateway Science Museum Community Advisory Board. She continues to be active in both of these organizations. She received the Paul Harris Award from Rotary and the Athena Service Award.

I told Judy I would write the first segment of this chapter; after that, she is entirely on her own to describe her class presentations and any lessons appertaining thereto. Her comma placement is much better than mine. Judy, *take it!*

This is Judy, and I am delighted to be able to share with you directly as the author of this chapter. Nothing gives me greater satisfaction, joy, and fulfillment than to talk about three of my greatest passions in life that have touched me and others personally and professionally and continue to do so. These passions are the acts of giving and kindness coupled with gratitude; providing exceptional service to others not only as customers but as friends and family; and recognizing and honoring those in your life, whether they are employees, friends, or family, by encouraging engagement in their passions and taking interest in all they do.

***Lesson: Explore and develop your passions in life; the outcome will bring great personal happiness and satisfaction.***

I wore many hats at Bi-Tech, and as Gary pointed out, these responsibilities evolved to an even greater magnitude as the company grew. One major task that has always been before me was the desire to provide exceptional customer service. This is key to the success of your company, as it was to ours. You can have an outstanding product, lovely work environment, super employees, and energetic marketing, but your company will not survive without exceptional customer service. So, keep it at the top of your list to focus on in your business and personal development.

Serving customers covers a wide spectrum of responsibilities, experiences, and actions. It involves problem solving, working through complex situations, and dealing with angry and frustrated clients and employees. It also involves creating fixes and sharing what can't be done within the scope of an application. Provide options and alternatives; encourage and address those who can't communicate well; answer questions simply and clearly; turn a negative situation into a positive one; and time after time work "magic" to create satisfaction.

At one time, customer service was considered a low-level position in a company. It wasn't a priority. The customer was second to many other aspects of the business. Those who provided service did not have lofty titles, pay, or a future. Other positions held glitzy, administrative titles; were considered crucial to the success of the company; and received enhanced compensation, benefits, and recognition. Customer service was a dead-end street with no way to climb the position ladder in a company; and in turn, added extensive overhead, time, and grief to the financial condition of the business.

In the eighties business gurus began to notice something important. Companies that worked hard to provide exceptional customer service had advantages and greater success overall. Their financial picture was brighter, they were more profitable and had fewer expenses related to client and product satisfaction, they experienced great growth and had repeat business, and they were more apt to be referenced as the company of choice.

So customer service bubbled to the top of the priorities on the path to success. The mantra became "create a memorable experience for each customer; meet or ideally exceed their expectations and satisfy their needs."

I've used many books to provide background and practical how-to guidelines on providing excellent customer service. The one that has had a great influence in my organizational planning for exceptional customer service is titled *Delivering Knock Your Socks Off Service,* by Kristin Anderson and Ron Zemke. This book is an excellent example of how to do it right.

Providing exceptional customer service should be intuitive, as it centers on life's principle of treating others as you wish to be treated. But, like many principles in life, it takes training, leadership, common sense, and work ethic, along with patience, compassion, and understanding. These are all very thoughtful characteristics that you don't always see in the workplace. So let's start with the basics of customer service.

The framework that is introduced in *Delivering Knock Your Socks Off Service* was created by Texas A&M researcher Dr. Leonard Berry and his colleagues at Texas A&M University. Dr. Berry found that customers evaluate customer service based on five factors, represented by the acronym **RATER:**

- **Reliability**: *Provide what was promised dependably and accurately.* Keep organization commitments, common expectations, and personal promises. Fulfill obligations.
- **Assurance**: *Show trust, confidence, competence, and courtesy. Smile.* Have product knowledge, company knowledge, listening skills, problem-solving skills, and style. "I can and want to help you ..."
- **Tangibles**: *Importance of physical plant, equipment, and your presentable style.* Demonstrate value. "From the customer's point of view, if they can see it, walk on it, hold it, hear it, step in it, smell it, carry it, step over it, touch it, use it, even taste it, if they can feel it or sense it, it's customer service" (from "Super American Training Program", pg. 27 of *Delivering Knock Your Socks Off Service*).
- **Empathy**: *Ability to care and provide individual attention.* People don't want to talk to a computer; they want to talk to a "real"

person. Acknowledge and affirm the customer. Build a good solid relationship with the person you're serving; be clear and timely. Walking in others' shoes is a sensitive approach to deal with their issue.

- **Responsiveness**: *Willingness to offer support and assistance promptly and with excellent follow-up.* Setting and meeting deadlines, and what to do when a customer must wait.

***Lesson: RATER should be top-of-mind in providing exceptional service.***

Reaffirming that a customer is right and addressing their needs in a timely fashion are paramount in a successful vendor/client relationship. Whether the client is right or wrong, excellent customer service thrives on not pointing fingers. Acknowledge that you understand how the problem occurred and how you're prepared to address it. Look for teaching moments and guide the customer along with you toward a resolution. Recognize that you appreciate hearing about the problem firsthand so that it can be fixed. Have the customer as your partner in achieving a solution.

Establishing trust is at the core of all lasting business relationships. To provide this foundation with and for your customer, you must communicate frequently, tell the truth, develop openness, show warmth and confidence, and keep promises. Customers respect honesty, whether the news you bring them is good or not-so-good.

Trust can be broken in ways other than being dishonest. A customer may feel vulnerable due to lack of information, expertise, or freedom to make changes, or feeling there is no recourse to a situation. Try to determine the reason for the customer's hesitancy and discomfort; fix whatever you can; and never hesitate to say "I'm sorry." Trust can be restored and in many cases be stronger than ever before.

***Lesson: Without trust, the customer/vendor relationship will be a dismal failure.***

However you are providing your customer service and building a relationship based on trust, whether it is face-to-face or remotely, there are practices that differentiate exceptional service from mediocre to poor service. Most importantly, you need to be a good listener.

## Sh-h-h, Listen, Question, and Respond

Throughout the process of serving your customers, being an "aggressive" listener will make your job and theirs much easier. Figure out what your customer wants by carefully following their conversation. Most of us hear only a fraction of what is being asked of us. To prevent misunderstandings and errors, write down the customer's key points and highlight those that truly capture the message. Ask additional questions of the customer to clarify and read back critical information. Gather clues by trying to read between the lines, as sometimes people have difficulty expressing themselves. Try to beat the statistic of most of us listening to only about 25 percent of what we hear.

Some of the items below become obstacles to effective listening:

- Your mind is elsewhere: Focus on the customer. Minimize outside distractions, noise, and interruptions.
- Be conscious of your attitude: Positive always wins. Negative intensifies not only the problem but the nature of the total customer experience. Be courteous and *smile*. Look at the cup as half-full, not half-empty.
- Initial words or phrases: Be open, cordial, friendly, and informative from the get-go. Making a favorable first impression will enhance the relationship and set a course for future productive contacts.
- Technology: The inability to be face-to-face with the customer can undermine the service provided if you're paying more attention to the technology surrounding you than listening to their request.

***Lesson: Listening with focus will enhance your customer/vendor experience.***

Along with listening, asking questions and requesting elaboration can further clarify the customer's need for service. The customer's contact may take the following course of action:

- **Getting Started with the Customer**: After your introduction and that of the customer, begin to collect or reconfirm existing pertinent data to address whatever their request might be. Verify their contact information; gather any details about their system configuration and software version. Repeat back their responses to verify that you have heard them correctly. Take down an accurate account of the nature of their call and prepare them to understand the steps you'll need to take toward a resolution. Close by sharing with them how you plan to follow up with their open issue.
- **Asking Open Questions**: These are questions that result in a more elaborate response. They allow you to gather details, answer additional questions or ask for greater clarification, and give you a greater opportunity to uncover the source of the client's problem.
- **Use of Closed Questions:** These are simply questions where the response can be yes or no or result in a single concrete response. Certainly such questions have their place in information gathering, but will not get to the depth of the issue like an open question may.
- **Ending Your Customer Contact**: You may want to highlight the major points made in the call and reinforce the plan for how you will manage the outcome. Follow-up is one of the more difficult tasks to track, especially when you don't have an immediate solution to the customer's problem at hand. Ensure that whatever you set as a plan for follow-up is managed appropriately. If you can't solve the problem according to the prescribed time line, notify the customer and continue notifying him or her with updates. Don't let the customer off your radar until the reason for the contact is resolved. And even then, you may want to follow up a week or so later to ensure the continued success of the fix and also to thank him or her for being such a good customer.

Managing a successful service call can be an art. You want to recognize the importance of the customer; customers are the reason you stay in business and have a job. Plus, it's the right thing to do! Putting them at ease throughout the contact, reassuring them that you will follow up appropriately, and reaffirming that their issue is important to you will go a long way to having a satisfied experience.

Good listening skills, questions to gain further clarification, and winning phrases all combine to produce an exceptional customer experience. A few examples of simple inappropriate introductory phrases spoken by a customer service representative are listed below, along with their positive and productive counterparts.

| **Instead of ...** | **Say ...** |
|---|---|
| "That's not the way it works." | "Try this as a possible solution." |
| "It's not my department." | "I will make every effort to solve your problem." |
| "You must do the following ..." | "I can help you proceed with the next step." |
| "It's in the *User Guide*." | "Let me take you to where a solution is documented." |
| "Hang on; wait a minute." | "May I put you on hold? Otherwise, I can call you back." |
| "I can't fix your problem now." | "It will take me a bit of time to research a solution; I will contact you in thirty minutes. Is that satisfactory?" |
| "This is not a high-priority issue." | "Your issue is important to me." |

***Lesson: Positive words/phrases set the tone for productive service communication.***

## Remote Customer Service

Many of your customer service requests come over the phone, by e-mail, in a text, or through social media. When these methods are used, you must accept the responsibility to ensure that the caller is satisfied regardless of the issue. Be aware of the behaviors and actions below when handling remote calls:

- **Answer the Phone**: Try to catch the call on the second or third ring and be prepared to respond the moment you pick up the receiver.
- **Giving Information**: Make sure you initially communicate a greeting, identify yourself, and ask how you can be of assistance.
- **Putting a Customer on Hold**: Ask if you may do that or call him or her back. If you anticipate an extended hold, make sure you come back on the line periodically so he or she knows you haven't dropped the call. Take messages; get the full name, phone number, and company name (spelled correctly); and make sure he or she has your name accurately. Read the contact information back.
- **Voice Mail**: A supplement to, not a replacement for, a service call. The first choice is to take the call. If a call does go to voice mail, listen to your messages frequently and return a call ASAP.
- **Conference Calls**: Communicate in an orderly fashion. Have a leader to address those on the call and pause before speaking.
- **Transferring a Call**: Try not to do it. But if you do, make sure the customer knows who he or she is going to, and also make sure the person you're transferring to knows the same. Stay on the line if you can to ensure the transfer occurs successfully and then sign off (a common practice for American Express).

***Lesson: Your mood comes through a call; smile—they can hear it in your voice.***

Customer service through e-mail can make or break a business's reputation. Although e-mail customer service is utilized by over half of the consumers who contact organizations for help, a bad e-mail can take on a life of its own. If you're using this method to address a customer issue, consider the following:

- Use e-mail to confirm an understanding, including details, responses to questions, and actions.
- Reinforce a relationship with an e-mailed thank-you note of recognition or sharing a point of interest or importance from a discussion. Use a method of documentation that reiterates an action plan, a verbal summary, or a clarification.
- Generally, don't e-mail when you're emotional; read your e-mail before sending; and respond promptly, courteously, and succinctly. Ensure that you're sending your e-mail to the correct person.

And lastly, before we actually look at face-to-face customer service, let's consider social media. There are positive and negative effects as a result of using Facebook, Twitter, LinkedIn, and other services. Positively, it allows people to connect in a convenient way among many and builds relationships; it reduces communication obstacles as you can address multiple topics with a larger group; and it provides a venue where business opportunities are easily updated and marketing activities can occur. Negatively, it can be addictive, can create isolation, and affects productivity, which can result in a loss of revenue.

## Face-to-Face Customer Service

To conclude the manner of communicating customer service, there's nothing to replace a face-to-face approach. The Walmart employee pledge reads, "I solemnly promise and declare that for every customer that comes within ten feet of me, I will smile, look them in the eye, and greet them, so help me, Sam."

All of the qualities we've listed about exceptional service when you're not physically with the customer hold true and even more so when you are face-to-face. Nonverbal actions and behaviors can outweigh the impact of words in establishing a positive or negative service rep/customer contact. Nonverbal cues can affect customer service in the following ways:

- **Smile**: First and of foremost importance is a smile. This facial gesture makes you more approachable; reduces the physical and emotional distance between you and the customer; and is welcoming, warm, and endearing. A smile is not only important face-to-face but during any remote form of communication. If you're smiling, one can hear it in your voice, on paper, and in a message.
- **Eye Contact**: Right up there at the top of the list with a smile is eye contact. Let your eyes meet those of the customer; it ensures that you're focused on his or her importance and you are listening. Looking down or away is perceived as cold, nonattentive, and totally disinterested.
- **Physical Attributes**: Stand straight and poised; it exudes confidence. Be neat and clean; have well-cared-for nails, hair, and clothing; and don't slouch. Your physical qualities are representative of the pride in your well-being and the importance of your work.
- **Not Too Close; Not Too Far**: Be conscious of your body language and gestures. Extend your hand for a handshake; stand within chatting distance, not to where you have to raise your voice or whisper. Relax and offer a chair or suggest a short walk as you chat; move to somewhere that's more confidential if necessary. Make the customer feel welcome and that you have nothing but time to address his or her needs.

***Lesson: Pay attention to both verbal and nonverbal cues to ensure exceptional customer communication.***

## Pleases and Thank-Yous

Throughout your communication with a customer, manners make all the difference. Requesting information with a please or expressing a thank-you shows that you care and respect the customer's role in the relationship.

Give thanks

- at the close of a conversation;
- when someone has provided you with information;
- when a customer has gone above and beyond the call of duty;
- at any portion of the conversation where the customer has clarified a question, given an example, helped you with an issue, or just plain made the call instead of suffering in silence;
- for the customer's patience, and if the customer is angry, let him or her know that you appreciate him or her giving you a chance to work with him or her to correct the issue;
- when he or she positively references you, your work, your company, or your product(s); and
- during a checkup call once the customer need is resolved.

This is a short list of circumstances for thank-yous. The list could be endless, and the opportunities are many. Keep in mind all those who provide forms of service to you: your family, friends, coworkers, vendors, and strangers. Thank them! Also, pat yourself on the back for your commitment to appreciation and extend that to yourself for the life that you lead and the work that you do.

***Lesson: Thankfulness is at the heart of true appreciation for ourselves and others. Be grateful and express it!***

## Oops! You Blew It with Your Customer Service (or Lack Thereof!)

After all these steps, prompts, ideas, and suggestions for exceptional customer service, what do you do when your communication still "goes south"? How can you repair, recover, and restore a relationship that has been flawed? The goal is to once again regain the trust and positive working environment with a customer who is disappointed, disillusioned, or angry with the way he or she has been treated. At least be thankful that you get this chance, as opposed to having him or her walk away, never to return, cease the use of your product, or become a negative reference.

Some steps to consider for moving forward:

- **Apologize**: Regardless of who's at fault, say, "I'm sorry" and find a way to correct the issue.
- **Empathize**: Listen to the reason for the service malfunction and express that you understand the customer's displeasure and discontentment. Emphasize that you will stay with the customer until there is resolution and satisfaction. Identify with his or her pain.
- **Fix It**: Do whatever you can in an expedient fashion to correct the oops. Bring in a coworker or specialist who may have a more in-depth knowledge of the problem; contact the customer with frequent updates on the progress of the fix; and offer a work-around, if appropriate, while the repair is ongoing.
- **Follow Up**: You can never check with the customer too often when rectifying a need for service. Don't wait for major progress; keep him or her apprised along the way. Once the fix has been delivered and the customer is satisfied, call again to thank him or her for giving you and the company a second chance.

***Lesson: Never underestimate the power and positive effect of an apology.***

## Recognition

Recognition for employees, staff, family, and friends comes in all shapes and sizes; you can never give too much and you can never receive enough. We've had a glimpse of the importance of the thank-you and now we need to extend that expression in thoughtful and special ways.

Some of my favorite ways are

- a written thank-you note
- an e-mail, phone call, or text noting appreciation
- taking a coworker to lunch
- surprising someone with a gift certificate, candy, fruit basket, flowers, or balloons
- jotting down a note to a member of the employee's family noting your appreciation
- celebrating with a party and awards for excellence
- providing additional training and career development for an employee
- putting up a Brag Board of notes of gratitude
- establishing concierge services at your workplace: dry cleaning pickup and delivery, car maintenance, food truck stop, to name a few
- caring by walking around (CBWA). Engage in non-work-related conversation regarding an employee's interests, activities, hobbies, and family life. Take notes after the conversation. Use your notes as ideas to customize your recognition.
- organizing seasonal parties and picnics
- holding a weekly fifteen-minute meeting where an employee is recognized and rewarded before his or her peers
- honoring birthdays, anniversaries, graduations, and other special events. Time permitting, attending a function where an employee or family member is being recognized.
- having fun with competitive contests among departments to build camaraderie and spirit
- participating in team sports and tournaments

- providing impromptu pizza parties, ice cream days, a Thanksgiving feast, Halloween trick or treating, and an Easter egg hunt. Include children and other family members in activities that create memories, a legacy, and traditions for your employees to enjoy.
- lunching with the CEO
- decorating with inspirational posters, images, and quotes
- sharing stories of excellence about employees
- publishing photos, newsletters, or banners recognizing employees
- organizing groups to adopt a less-fortunate family by providing necessities and treats

There are many books and articles dedicated to ways of recognizing others. My list is just the tip of the iceberg. My favorite way to recognize is to make it a surprise, when it's least expected. Your recognition should always be thoughtful, timely, sincere, and with respect for the individual you're honoring. Recognition brings joy to your employees and to the workplace. It creates a bond of appreciation and caring, promotes employee engagement, and is contagious. For some it's a natural behavior to recognize, and others will learn by modeling your behavior. No need to wait for *big* reasons to recognize. Take it in small steps, every day, in a variety of ways, providing a culture of appreciation and celebration for all!

***Lesson: Recognition is more than the icing on the cake—it's the whole cake!***

Thus, we end Judy's chapter. If you are just starting out or have a going concern, you would be well served to read this chapter multiple times. Happy employees and happy customers are the cornerstones of success. Thank you, Judy.

DEVILS TOWER TRADING POST

# 5

# Research and Development: This Meeting Is for What?

James Bennett

When I asked James to write a brief biography for his presentation to the class, he offered the following: "Came to Chico State many moons ago; joined Bi-Tech as a sophomore and never left. During his tenure, he has created software with lots of bugs, ported to platforms that are no longer in business, removed databases during a live demo, sent anonymous notes from airport fax machines, traveled on "consulting" junkets to Paris, Milan, and London, got seriously lost in Texas, froze his butt off in Ville de Pierrefonds, Canada, panicked at user conferences, and ran the boss's Harley out of gas.

"In between he created some software, supported and trained on the same, did technical demos, contract negotiations, and product management; managed the IT and 'cloud' team, and before sanity gained the upper hand, managed over 120 people in QA, development, and documentation, spanning more time zones and countries than he wants to recall.

"He doesn't drink very much, but probably should start."

As I said in my chapter, I met James as a student in my database management class in the eighties. Besides being remarkably brilliant, he was a bit of a smartass. When James was promoted to vice president of research and development, he became an invaluable member of the "executive" team.

In addition to being a software development wizard, James kept us focused when we held meetings. It was wonderful to watch him in a meeting. He would sit there quietly, and only offer comments when directly addressed. When the meeting was approaching its conclusion, James would ask, "What are we doing different as a result of this meeting?" This is the essence of James: cut through the BS and get real work done. By the way, his software had very few bugs. As can be told by his bio, he has a refreshing wit.

Because I have been out of the technical side for over fourteen years, I asked James to write this chapter. The text that follows contains some real-world nuggets for anyone wanting to do a technical startup. The following is in his words. Warning: James loves run-on sentences.

## Getting Started

A brief background on my history: My first exposure to a computer was an Apple IIe as a freshman in high school, followed by an Atari 800 in precalculus, where I was able to play around with basic graphing functions. Keep in mind this was a time when nobody really knew what to do with this mysterious box, and heaven forbid we had a substitute teacher because then "students are not allowed to play with expensive equipment!"

Somehow during my junior year, this experimentation culminated in our family acquiring a Radio Shack TRS-80 (48K of RAM and not one, but two, floppy drives!). My stepdad was a disk jockey and program manager for a local FM station and needed to create ad scheduling and billing software for the station. It was pretty fun, crammed into a small closet, writing Basic and Z-80 assembler and translating wish-list items into reality. And technically, it was my first startup, where I found that 10 percent of nothing is, well, nothing. ☺ While today everyone is blasé about what computers can do, this experience was the genesis of the joy I still find today when watching someone's face as you solve (by "magic") a vexing, annoying, or complicated problem.

***Lesson: Never forget you are there to solve a problem.***

I've come to find that most people in high school are really unsure of the path they wish to lead after graduation, but I confess I never had that problem. As a junior I sent a letter to IBM, HP, and DEC, asking where they went to recruit for computer science grads. From IBM, I received a glossy politically correct brochure that as near as I could tell never answered my question (but a job as a printer for IBM seemed lucrative); HP wrote me a two-paragraph response citing CalTech, Texas A&M, and Chico State as prime recruiting locations. One quick look at the tuition requirements kept me from viewing the likely ego-bruising entrance requirements for the other two, and it was off to Chico State for me.

I had one year in the dorm paid for and $600 in cash to get through the first year. Thus, pretty soon I was working at Burger King, and then as a dishwasher/prep cook at Mr. Steak, where among my more obvious duties, I was the "volunteer" to jump up and down in the dumpster doing my simulation of a redneck trash compactor.

***Lesson: Never pass up a real-world perspective.***

Some interesting side thoughts on my favorite courses at Chico State start with CSCI 59. Its purpose was to allow students to use a terminal for the HP1000 assembly language course instead of, gasp, punch cards. Nerd note: I still recall that memory location zero was also the Indirect Load Register (A?), and if you set only the high bit in this location and did the equivalent of "LD A, Indirect," the machine would lock up tighter than a, well, pick a metaphor. The best part of this class was that it was taught by a grad student who had finished an internship at HP. Once the class had concluded, he offered to meet in the same time slot/room and describe what it was like to actually have a "real job." I remember sitting there with a few others and just absorbing everything he said.

CSCI 280 (Compiler Theory) taught me that problems that seem really complicated (lexical analysis, code generation and optimization) can be simplified greatly with the right methodology and tools. When you run into something where you find yourself spewing days and thousands of lines of code at a problem, it often means you need to step back and rethink the problem.

CSCI 273 (Database Management), taught by Gary, introduced a whole new way to achieve order in a crazy world. And for the record, I'm sure Gary has a selective memory about some of my comments during class; surely I wasn't that flippant. [Gary's note: Yes, he was.] Later, much later, Gary would introduce me to Greg Wagstaff from the American Red Cross, where we were to present a proof of concept, with the opener, "If you don't like it, James is going to kick your butt." You frankly just never know what Gary is going to say! Never dull, though.

My transition to a real job occurred as I was running across campus (why are the hardest calculus classes always at 8:00 a.m.?) when I spied a Help Wanted ad for a computer job posted on a board at the Associated Students/University Foundation. A quick follow-up and then an interview with the head of accounting, Joyce Friedman, and lo and behold, Dr. Sitton, who apparently was running this system as a side job.

After Gary quizzed me with a few questions ("What does MPE stand for?" is all I recall), a few days passed, and I now had a job with a door, and my days of jumping up and down in dumpsters were over. It may have also helped that after my interview, I went around campus and removed all of the job postings from the boards; I was really tired of pants that stand up by themselves at the end of a workday.

Three months later, Gary called me and said, "You've never actually called me with any questions—not true; I managed to get the entire magnetic tape wound up on the take-up reel, and Gary had to drive down and fix it—how would you like an internship at Bi-Tech?" So the next semester I had two "real jobs" and learned the expensive lesson of having two W-2s with a student exemption!

Briefly put (ha), this is how I started, as a junior, a thirty-year (rounding up a bit) career with Bi-Tech and its successors. Starting as a developer, then a product manager, and eventually vice president of technology (or R & D or CTO, depending on my audience), and spanning lots of different incarnations of Bi-Tech: a small mom-and-pop shop (literally), a small company (today you paint the lines on the basketball court), one acquired by a Fortune 500 company, one in high-growth pre-Y2K mode, one that acquired a company (and later divested), and then eventually merged into other business units.

And, Dorothy, what have I learned on my trip down the Yellow Brick Road?

## People

The hiring process generally starts with a resume, which consumes an inordinate amount of time (for both the producer and consumer) but really provides very little benefit. There are a few core concepts that should be extracted from a resume: attention to detail (i.e., spelling, grammar, and ability to proofread one's own work), eligibility to work in the United States, whether the history and pace of switching companies matches your expectations and culture, and core technical mastery—for example, PMP certification for project managers, or a SQL Server DBA (database administrator) applying to an Oracle™ shop.

This basic filter allows you to separate a pile of resumes into two or three piles: Nope, Worth a follow-up call, and a "Maybe" pile. The interesting thing about the Maybe pile is that one of our best developers, Ray Potts, had no formal training in software development, one of our top system-level developers has his degree in communications, and our most experienced system administrator has a degree in music. Once you find a few of these exceptions (and exceptional people), you'll find your Maybe pile grows a tad.

***Lesson: Hire exceptional people, regardless of their degree.***

As to job history, understand that some people may have been consultants and retained for a fixed time or project duration, which is different than somebody who doesn't work out for whatever reason and moves on (voluntarily or otherwise). If it looks like there is a pattern of this short-term history, there are a couple of explanations: maybe the companies are all startups and flamed out, the aforementioned poor performer, or someone who is trying to aggressively fill his or her resume and climb up the ladder.

For the ladder climber, estimate how long it takes for a new employee to become productive and whether he or she is worth bringing on board if he or she will simply leave in eighteen to twenty-four months. In our world, where most of the interviewers have ten to twenty years of experience at the same company, we tend to not be too tolerant of those who flip jobs. Once we were five minutes into an interview, and the applicant flat out stated that he or she would be there less than two years. And that pretty much ended the interview.

***Lesson: Beware of short-term employment goals.***

Beyond core skills, any technical position requires good problem-solving skills, an aptitude for digging in and solving problems, and general communication skills. One way to assess this is with a behavioral interview, to explore how applicants have shown initiative or problem-solving skills in the past. If they claim to know SQL Server, ask them about the process they used to troubleshoot one of their toughest performance issues. Make sure you are clear what they actually did versus their team's work. Ask about a time they screwed up and how they recovered, what was communicated to their team/supervisor and the timing. Are there examples of when they articulated improvements to tools, processes, or designs? Was this improvement within their project or outside? The intent is to elicit responses that will describe *how* they do their job and interact with their peers and management.

There is a fundamental economic model at play with any employee. You must get more value out of their contribution than you are paying them. Payment is both direct in the form of cash and benefits and indirect in whatever form of angst and overhead they heap on you, their supervisor, their team, or the company. In effect, people who are poor performers (or cause enough drama to marginalize their production) are not sustainable. Your options are to address their issues by one or more of the following: coaching, finding them a new position, or firing them. This is mandatory and arguably the most important thing that you can do as a manager. And depending on your personality, the hardest to actually accomplish.

***Lesson: Always assess the indirect cost of an employee.***

As many of you will start your career as employees, I'll share a concept from a book I read many moons ago, *The Soul of a New Machine,* by Tracy Kidder. The book told the story of the culture, work ethic, and personalities of a small skunkworks project within Data General, building the Eclipse minicomputer. One of my takeaways from this book was a concept named "pinball," in that when you show up on any given day to work on your current project, you are actually applying for the next project. This philosophy is a great way to think about adding knowledge and skills as you work your way around a company.

***Lesson: Your current project is a training ground for your next project.***

The other is a takeaway from Agile Scrum training we had: When someone asks you a question, the answer is always in the form of "Yes, *and* ..." Even when your initial thought is "No, are you f—— kidding?" it can almost always be rephrased as "Yes, I can make that date, but only if we remove most of the features and skip the load testing." In other words, you are stating the conditions under which you can be successful, and even if those conditions can't be met, it keeps the door open for further discussion. And once you have a reputation for "Yes, *and*" responses, you'll find lots of doors opening.

***Lesson: Be a "Yes, and ..." employee.***

## Allen Curve

In the early days of Bi-Tech, we worked out of Gary and Judy's house, and in my case, with about a half dozen of us in one room with desks and not a "cube" in sight. This remains one of the most efficient and productive work arrangements I can recall. Have a problem? Just ask. Want to gloat over some new feature? Turn around and invite your coworker to take a peek. This is a high level of interaction that is very hard to duplicate with remote workers. In my case, I have employees who work two hundred feet from me, and on some days I have the same interaction with them that I do with those thousands of miles away.

The Allen curve (from MIT Professor Thomas J. Allen in the late seventies) shown below demonstrates the negative correlation between distance and frequency of communications. While one can quibble about the terms "*frequency* of communication" vs. "*quality* of communication," note that the X-axis of the curve is in *meters*, not miles. Wow!

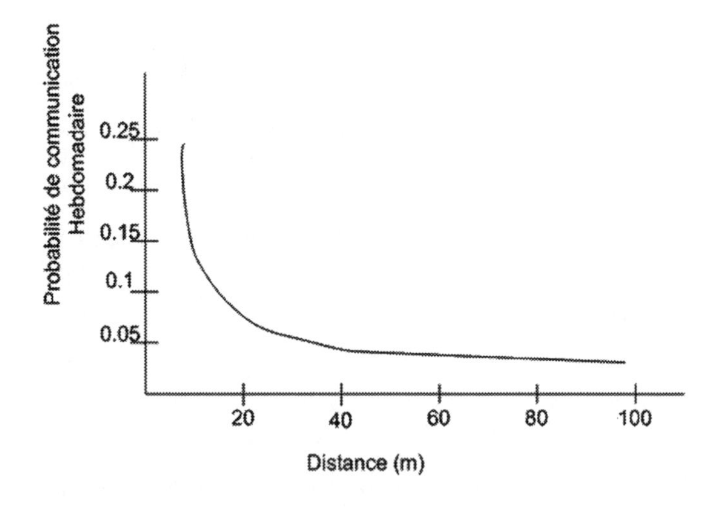


***Lesson: The frequency of communication is a function of distance.***

As a specific case, I'm sure you are familiar with the "meeting after the meeting." In other words, after the meeting has formally ended, a few people stick around and share those thoughts that they weren't willing (or didn't have time) to do earlier and they explore other avenues of thought. Arguably, this is the best part of the meeting, and if you are remote, you don't even get a chance to participate.

***Lesson: When meeting remotely, include the meeting after the meeting.***

The reality today, though, is that lots of people work from home, and if you are working for a multinational company with thousands of employees, they aren't going to be in the same room, much less within one hundred meters of each other. Having remote employees requires more management to keep the team aligned and on the same page. You need to take extra time to ensure that the "meetings after meetings" occur within the meeting, though you'll never be 100 percent successful.

## Culture

A company can develop a culture by happenstance, by design, or simply based on the characteristics of the leader/CEO. However it occurs, every company has a different culture. Whether it is dress code, the level of interaction with customers, or how it measures utilization, all companies are different.

When Bi-Tech was acquired, the interaction with our new parent was almost 100 percent through the CFO (Bruce) and president (Gary). Essentially, make your revenue and EBIDTA (earnings before interest, depreciation, taxes, and amortization) goals set at the beginning of the year, and they would leave you alone. One memory of the early discussions with our new boss was a notebook Gary created labeled "Synergy," with presumably lots of ideas on how we could leverage this new relationship to both of our benefits. The gentleman "from corporate" dismissed the idea (and may have just tossed the notebook in the trash) and stated "there is no synergy."

It seemed rude at the time, but after experiencing a few mergers (from both sides), I can state that this oft-touted "synergy" takes a huge amount of work and often sucks out all of your forward momentum in the market—a fact seized with glee by your competitors.

***Lesson: The acquiring company cares about EBIDTA, not synergy.***

When companies merge, you generally have a few facets: first, redundant positions are eliminated almost exclusively in favor of the dominant partner (with the immediate generation of resentment on the other side); second, a revamped product road map is created, which tends to emphasize integration over features; and third, there is an inevitable culture clash of all sorts of intangibles, for example, summer picnics, user conferences, and dress code. This clash is very often not directly addressed and simply festers under the surface for years.

In an ideal world, a steering committee would be formed with equal participants to act as a funnel and decision-making body for all of the cultural issues that arise. Normally, I'm not a big fan of committees, but in this case having a formal process to ensure that voices are heard and decisions recorded and communicated is very helpful to ensure forward progress.

***Lesson: A steering committee can help defuse culture clashes.***

And culture issues can arise without any merger and acquisition activity; we had customers in both New York City and the "South." The former would start a full verbal assault over what seemed like minor issues, and the latter would be apple-pie sweet all the time, even when they announced they were leaving for your competition because you had not been paying attention. Both are very emotional interactions, and it's easy to let them hamper your critical-thinking processes.

The most dramatic cultural introduction occurred when we started outsourcing to India. Beyond the very painful twelve-and-a-half- (or thirteen-and-a-half-) hour time difference, we found it very difficult to achieve the desired level of productivity. In time we got better, but there are some things we should have done better.

First, we should have sent a few employees to live in India for eighteen to twenty-four months at a stretch. We tried to make do with quarterly visits of a few weeks' duration, but Allen's curve is fully engaged at this point. There is no substitute for somebody with his or her butt planted at the site who can be the liaison among matters of product, policy, procedures, and culture. Otherwise you have a communication path that is in twenty-four-hour cycles: an e-mail is sent at 9:00 a.m. IST (India) time (or 8:30 p.m. Pacific), and since most people are in TV mode by then, the response doesn't come back until 8:00 a.m. Pacific or 8:30 p.m. IST. So what would be a five-minute conversation in person is now a two-day ordeal.

***Lesson: Time-zone differences can take two days for a five-minute conversation.***

Second, even though our staff in India spoke English, the dialect was sometimes hard to understand. If you were directly involved with India, you would pick it up quickly enough, but for employees who interacted on an infrequent basis, it was a huge impediment. About five years into our effort, we found that there is "dialect training" to help address this. Not for us stateside, though, which was too bad, because I was really hoping to pick up a Texas accent.

***Lesson: Dialect training can help with offshore communications.***

Third, the employment cycle is quite a bit different in India than in the United States. It would take months to hire people, primarily because instead of the two-week notice period common in the United States, it was a multiple-month exit process in India. Usually the people you want to hire are already employed, which, when coupled with a three- to six-week recruitment process, easily meant you were waiting three months for new hires. And of course, the holidays are different, which is obvious when you think about it but always a surprise the first time around.

***Lesson: Recruitment in India takes longer, and they have different holidays.***

Fourth, the network latency (not the bandwidth) between two places at opposite ends of the earth is dramatic. We had to ramp up servers in India, as well as Citrix environments in the States, to provide work environments that performed roughly equivalent to what we would see locally.

Fifth, our recruiting efforts somehow inadequately addressed the fact that most of our work was of the maintenance variety, and we experienced very high turnover (25–35 percent) for the first few years until we figured this out.

Finally, we (both the United States and India staff) undertook a cultural-awareness training, which sounds very Kumbaya-ish, but it was actually very effective in understanding the different paradigms at work in the two cultures. If nothing else, simply admitting there were differences and that they were causing problems was a big benefit. For instance, in the States we tend to be more egalitarian, with relatively flat management structures, and in India, at least with our team there, it was very hierarchical, which made "team" meetings seem very flat and one-sided.

***Lesson: Cultural-awareness training actually helps.***

## Beware What's Below the Waterline

The first iteration of the Bi-Tech product that I was aware of ran on a Hewlett-Packard 3000, and everything you needed to run this product was available from HP: compiler, database, user interface, everything. If a customer had an HP3000, everything you needed for your application to run was there, ready to go. More importantly, the lines of support were clearly drawn. The customer *always* had a maintenance contract with HP, and they would handle operating-system and hardware issues, and we dealt with the application software problems.

Compare that with today, where a developer who wants to create an application that runs on a desktop must contend with a horde of different operating systems, patches, printer and network drivers, and antivirus software, to name a few. Honestly, it is amazing anything runs at all!

The point here is that when you create your app, you think you'll only have to support the code you wrote. The reality is that you are providing a solution, and that solution has many touch points outside of your control. None of these touch points has as friendly a support staff as your company (right?), so guess who gets all of the calls.

My "favorite" was a problem where a laser printer had a bad memory card, and therefore charts/graphs that we were printing over a certain size would produce gibberish. Was this technically "our" problem? Well, on the one hand, no, we don't sell printers or memory cards, but on the other, Mr. Muckity-Muck needs his graph for his City Council meeting that night and clicked *our* print button and it didn't print, so who is he going to call?

All this is to say that when you think of creating, say, a mobile app, and for cash reasons, you are forced to choose between iOS™ and Android™, think of all of the combinations of Android platforms and how you will certify those as compared to the same situation in iOS. Obviously the world is more complicated than just this one criterion, but consider where you want to spend your effort. For our ERP (enterprise resource planning) market, which differs considerably from the consumer world, we can afford to be very explicit about versions and platforms we support to avoid this quagmire. And it still bites us.

***Lesson: Your solution involves your code, plus a great deal more.***

## Technical Debt

The first generation of a product allows you to choose from a wide-open field (or greenfield) of options. You can choose the architecture, the components, the UI (user interface) design, the security model, frameworks, and many other aspects. However, you really only get to do this once; then it is really maintenance from that point forward. It is easy to convince yourself that you do a revolutionary overhaul at any time, but rarely do you have the time and capital necessary for such an endeavor. What you end up with is a lot of technical debt.

Simply put, technical debt is comprised of two things. The most pernicious is that annoying section of code that you are always going to rewrite because it is a support nightmare, but solving that problem is (a) expensive and (b) not going to generate you any new revenue. So it never gets done.

The second form of technical debt is that forced upon you by your partners. If your app runs on iOS and Apple releases version N+1, you are immediately in debt, and you will have to direct resources appropriately to ensure that your customers can upgrade on their schedule, not yours.

***Lesson: Technical debt is an inevitable outcome of product development.***

A year or so ago, we wrote a mobile app based on HTML5 and used various third-party and open-source products, including jQuery, jQuery Mobile, SignalR, Infragistics, and PhoneGap. We used all these products because it accelerated our time to market and allowed us to focus on our core competency without having to code everything from scratch.

We released the product, the crowd went wild, orders were rolling, and ... poof! Apple released a new version of iOS. And so it began: we needed to update both Infragistics and jQuery because they had tweaks to support the new platform, and this caused a ripple effect and pretty soon every external dependency was being updated. And of course, all of these vendors hadn't found all of the bugs either, so now you are creating bug reports for them, getting beta releases, and bemoaning their inability to meet their deadlines so you can meet *your* deadlines. Damn software companies.

Actually, running on the latest platform is a feature, even though it doesn't seem like it. If you are lucky, you can see these changes coming; otherwise, you will have an adverse impact on your road map and customer commitments.

***Lesson: You must schedule realistic estimates to address technical-debt issues.***

Proof: As I said earlier, when I started at Bi-Tech, we ran on an HP3000, using COBOL, and under the IMAGE database management system. From there we migrated to C/UNIX/Informix, then UNIX/Oracle, and then Windows/SQL Server/C++/C#, but still have about 40 percent of the original COBOL code. Of course, we were able to do this transition because we wrote, in effect, an HP batch processor, spooler, API (application programming interface) emulator, and a database layer that made UNIX look like an HP3000. Why? Because a rewrite to create a native UNIX app would have been too expensive and time-consuming. And when we moved to Windows, we made Windows look like UNIX (which looked like an HP3000). It was always the plan to rewrite this layer of code and some of it has happened over the years, but there are still some remnants of this approach today.

## Convention over Configuration

One of the challenges with software design is to understand whether product options need to exist to support the different needs of the market, as compared to individual desires either internal or external. In our market, this is further complicated by various regulatory requirements or union/enterprise policies.

The number of configuration settings causes numerous challenges: initial setup can be daunting and hard to support; testing the various unique combinations is exhaustive/exhausting and often impractical; and of course, creating and maintaining code with complex configuration drivers is a recipe for buggy software.

At one point, I calculated the number of different code paths for accepting a single record, and conservatively the number was over a thousand. This for a product that had about two hundred customers. While unit testing can address some of this, it would be best to avoid this situation altogether.

Convention over configuration is a paradigm for frameworks to simplify their implementation by making (and enforcing) assumptions about how the product will be used and allowing only limited or constrained exceptions. This concept can be extended to the solution itself by acknowledging that most options are driven by a lack of understanding of how the product will be used or an overly influential product manager or customer. Whenever possible, in the absence of good market data on the need for an option, put in a reasonable default and defer the need for an option to later. If you can ingrain a culture of options being the exception rather than the rule, you will find life a lot easier in the long run.

***Lesson: Software options are confusing, expensive, and difficult to support.***

## Cloud vs. On-Premise

Cloud infrastructure and application hosting have grown dramatically in the last few years, and given the plethora of material out there already, I'll simply add a few comments. I believe it is effectively impossible to create an application that is successful on-premise and will scale as desired in the cloud. On-premise apps need to conform to the needs and skills of the in-house staff who will maintain them, and this leads you to use market-acceptable components and architectures.

For a cloud-only solution, you are free to focus on delivering a product that uses the best tools possible regardless of the "religious" preferences of the selection committee or the knowledge base of the staff.

For example, to deliver an on-premise solution today that requires a database, the odds are very likely that you will use SQL Server or perhaps Oracle. For cloud-only, MySQL or any of the NoSQL solutions (MongoDB, CouchDB, etc.) are suddenly viable options, and you can choose freely to minimize your costs and improve the final value of the product.

Switching perspectives for a moment, if you are a consumer of a cloud-based product, make sure you understand who has ownership of the data, that you can extract it if necessary should the nature of the relationship change, that any regulatory or compliance directives you must respect are a part of the SLA (service-level agreement) with your provider, and that your disaster recovery plans (and testing!) include this component.

For multinational companies, hosting of employee or customer data has significant implications regarding data privacy; getting timely advice on the relevant issues here will save you lots of time and money in the future.

***Lesson: Cloud development wins; however, understand the SLA (service-level agreement) and get advice on data privacy.***

As to infrastructure-as-a-service, while much has been made of the cost and time efficiencies as well as moving some of your largest capital expenses to the operational side of the ledger, make sure the real problem you are solving isn't simply an internal approval process that can't keep pace. If they can't keep up due to the complexities of various policies, you should consider whether the primary driver of moving to the cloud is bypassing these requirements, and if so, maybe those policies should be reviewed or abandoned.

***Lesson: Internal policies need to keep pace with internal approval requirements.***

## API and Tools

One way to both provide convention-over-configuration and maintain the customizability and extensibility desired by customers is to expose key processes or data via an API (application programming interface). This provides a clean demarcation line as to where your software support ends, while still providing a model that will empower sufficiently savvy customers. We've used this model to allow customers to leverage their existing data and back-end processes with their own mobile applications and web forms.

Beyond a programmatic API, consider exposing a scripting model for high-configurations areas. In our case, payroll calculations can vary from the simple to the complex, and some financial reports can involve very complicated conditional logic. In both of these cases, we provided scripting support to allow customers to add their own levels of complexity. It does introduce considerable challenges on the support side, but sometimes it can't be helped.

Providing a way to extend the software and empower the customer to craft their own bolt-on solutions helps to ensure a satisfied customer and ensure that your product is focused on features applicable to the general marketplace rather than one-off customer solutions.

***Lesson: An API and scripting help savvy users, not the help desk.***

## Troubleshooting

Developers today are very familiar with integrated debugging, setting breakpoints, being able to examine variables, and all the other accoutrements of the modern development environment. Almost all of these disappear when the application goes into production. Inevitably, the software will not work as the customer expects, and the code must absolutely support some type of logging operation to allow you to determine if it is a bug or possibly some obscure system setting.

In addition, there are applications that will instrument your code and "phone home" unhandled exceptions, most common code paths, and general usage. Consider leveraging these tools because they give you unparalleled insight into how your application is actually being used. Consider what you would do if you knew that one of your more labor-intensive features was dramatically underused. Is it because people don't know it is there? Is the UI too obtuse? Is it not performing well? Having data that will help you answer these questions is invaluable.

If you use Windows, you are familiar with Microsoft's dialog that will ask you to "Check for Solutions" or "Submit an Error" when an app has a problem. If you write code for Windows, register your application (EXE and DLLs) with Microsoft, and they will share with you specific error occurrences and even allow you to request minidumps of the faulting process. This allows you to address problems that aren't even reported to you.

Finally, error messages should include both a unique numeric identifier and enough information to assist the user, support staff, or developer. The numeric identifier helps because it then becomes the referential search term when looking for a solution. Also, too often one sees an error message that is very vague, and with even a minor amount of specific information, it would assist the end user or support staff immensely.

***Lesson: Examine all methods to detect and report errors.***

James, you did a wonderful job of writing your own chapter. It was informative and very entertaining. I have no idea what the editor will do to your run-on sentences; I hope nothing. Thank you, James. I O U one!

# 6

# The CFO Duties: Finding Your Niche

Bruce Langston

When Bi-Tech was really starting to grow and I saw the light about hiring a marketing and sales person, we also knew we needed "real" accountants to help with implementations. Our vice president for marketing suggested an old CSU, Chico, friend of his, Bruce Langston. Bruce had the right credentials, and he was both a CPA and great working with people. We hired Bruce in January 1990 to do system implementations.

As the company continued to grow, Bruce finally convinced Judy and me that we needed a controller. Boy, was he right; and boy, was he good at it! Bruce's greatest skill was the ability to squirrel away money. At the end of the year when I needed to buy some hardware, I would go to Bruce. He always found a way to fund these important purchases. I used to say, "So, Bruce, what's our number?" to which he would answer, "What do you want it to be?"

As stated in my chapter, Bruce was the key player during the due diligence of the SunGard acquisition of Bi-Tech. He so impressed the people at SunGard they made him "group CFO"; that was a really big deal, and it put Bruce on the front lines of some very large acquisitions.

Bruce's presentation was the most surprising. I fully expected to see many PowerPoint slides of financial statements and organization charts. Instead, he gave an amazing oral recount of his career, with some real gems for the aspiring entrepreneur. Bruce never showed one slide, he rarely referred to his notes, he wrote a few things on the whiteboard, he talked for the entire 110 minutes, and the students loved his presentation. His chapter was the easiest; I simply copied his well-thought-out notes and pasted them, with some simple editing.

## Good Morning

My name is Bruce Langston. I am a CSU—or Chico State, as we like to call it—graduate from 1977. I was a business major, with a concentration in accounting. I have a CPA license and have held several accounting-related positions both before and after graduation. As I go through this presentation, I'll pause occasionally to see if you have any questions at that point. However, feel free to ask me a question or make your own comment at any time. I'd really rather this be more conversational than me just reading through this presentation.

## How I Got Here

I think one of the points Gary wants me to get across to you is how I got here. How was I able to achieve the success that I've had, so that perhaps you can use my experiences to help you achieve success in your career? If you will indulge me a bit, I'll kind of give you my accounting life story.

I discovered, by accident, early on (in high school, actually) that I had a knack for accounting. Back then it was bookkeeping, really. I needed electives in high school, so I took a bookkeeping class. It was one of those individualized learning–type classes, where you have modules to complete and can go at your own pace. I finished all the modules in less than half a semester with an A. This meant I now had a class period that I did not need to attend, which was great. So the next semester I took the advanced bookkeeping class, along with a few other business-type electives, and the same thing happened. Not only were these classes easy for me, but I actually enjoyed them. So from that point forward, I was a business major.

***Lesson: Find what you're good at and stick with it.***

From high school I went to a junior college, then on to Chico State. All through JC and Chico, I had various part-time jobs. My senior year at Chico, I landed a job at the Bar X liquor store on Ninth and Main as a clerk. I wanted that job very badly. I had a roommate who worked there, I would get a discount on beer, and lots of coeds frequented the store. I bugged the manager every day for weeks until he finally hired me.

Little did I know at the time that would be the job that would launch my accounting career. You see, a block up Ninth Street, there was a small CPA office. The CPA who owned it, Roger Sheldon, would frequently come into Bar X to buy smokes, cash a check, buy beer, or whatever. We became friends and had some interesting "accounting"-type conversations. During my last semester at Chico, which coincided with tax season, he asked me if I wanted some part-time work doing the write-up work for some of his tax clients. Of course, I took him up on it and landed my first "real job" in accounting.

***Lesson: Recognize opportunity and jump on it.***

Looking back, this was a decision that helped shape my entire accounting career going forward. Working with Roger, I had hands-on first-person experience with his clients: farmers, small business owners, some well-established, some just starting out. I saw every aspect of their business from an accounting perspective: sales, expenses, draws, loans, taxes of all types, everything. I saw those businesses that were successful and those that weren't so successful. Often not so much the business, as the way it was run or managed, had a lot to do with the success. A business that failed could have easily succeeded with a different approach to operating the business.

Remember that good employees are much less likely to leave a business that is performing poorly than they are to leave because of poorly performing management. Since Roger's business could not really afford me on a full-time basis, I looked for other opportunities.

***Lesson: Management is a key ingredient to employee retention and a successful business.***

## A Turning Point

Should I take my degree and a little bit of experience and head off to the big city and presumably the big bucks, or try to stay in Chico? I opted to stay in Chico. I landed another job at Davis Hammond and Co. in Oroville, which was a well-known regional CPA firm that performed a lot of audits on not-for-profits: school districts, water districts, small cities, and block grants. I got my audit experience for my CPA license. However, I didn't like Oroville or the commute very much, so I left.

***Lesson: If you don't like where you are, move on.***

I went back to Roger and asked if I could try to build up his business by bringing on more clients. He agreed, and I was fairly successful in bringing in more small business clients. Not too long afterward, he sold the business to two CPAs, and that firm became Levine & Collado, CPAs here in Chico. Besides Roger's clients, they wanted me in the deal. So I transitioned to them and continued to work with small businesses and farmers in the Chico area for the next ten years or so. I did take a brief two-year stint in Long Beach at another CPA firm. I felt I needed to see if I could succeed somewhere other than Chico. Sometimes you need to test yourself, which is what I was really doing in Southern California.

***Lesson: Sometimes you need to test yourself on a bigger stage.***

My time in Southern California was important because I met my future wife there; however, I didn't like the firm very much, and other than the recreation, I didn't like Southern California very much. I had moved there at the urging of a college buddy who had relocated down there. He was selling HP hardware in the higher-education segment. As it turned out, he and Gary were meeting up at demos where he had the hardware and Gary had the software for these education-type prospects.

After some courtship, Gary hired him as his sales manager, and he suggested me to fill an implementation manager position at Bi-Tech. I was to work with the finance types at schools, cities, and counties that had licensed the Bi-Tech software products and needed implementation assistance.

## The Stars Aligned

After I met with Gary and Judy in Chico, they offered me the position, and I jumped on it! So back to Chico, out of public accounting, which I was getting tired of, and into a whole new type of work. But remember my audit experience with not-for-profits? Perfect. Remember my experience working with small businesses and recognizing good manager/owners from poor ones? Perfect.

I continued in the implementation manager role for several years, all the while thinking that this great company, growing like crazy, really needed an in-house controller. I pestered Gary and Judy about this from time to time, and one day they agreed.

I soon found out that their plan was to sell the company to SunGard. I quickly put together a more formal accounting department, added some staff, added internal controls, beefed up the recording and reporting of transactions, and brought our books into conformity with GAAP (Generally Accepted Accounting Principles). I was again drawing on my education and experience working with small businesses and my CPA training.

Going through the SunGard acquisition was another great learning experience. I learned an enormous amount about GAAP for publicly traded software companies. I worked with some very experienced and smart accountants at SunGard. We all found that there were some great leaders at SunGard, and we learned a great deal about how a big multinational company operates.

As SunGard continued to expand the higher education and public sector group, I took on the role of group CFO. I worked on more than twenty acquisitions, not all of which consummated in actually acquiring the company. I oversaw the budgeting, constant re-forecasting, GAAP compliance, Sarbanes-Oxley compliance, tax compliance, public company reporting compliance, and everything else accounting-related for an ever-expanding number of business units within the group. I managed to stay based in Chico, but spent a large part of my time traveling around the United States and the United Kingdom.

## Another Turning Point

Then the recession of 2008/2009 happened. SunGard, which had gone private in a leveraged buyout in 2005, had to reorganize and get much leaner. "Do more with less" became the mantra. A large part of their business was with brokerage firms and banks, and we all know what happened to them.

So I left SunGard and had to make another decision on whether to leave or stay in Chico. The decision was not difficult. So for the last five years, I've been kind of an accounting "fix-it" man. I helped Fifth Sun get their accounting department and systems organized and compliant with their bank covenants. I helped Auctiva transition to the world of corporate ownership and public company requirements when they were purchased by Alibaba.com. I'm now at Cascade Orthopedic Supply, helping them deal with growing pains and bank oversight in a very tight-margin business.

So, there is my long-winded accounting life story. Here are some takeaways from all this: Find what you enjoy and stick with it. If you enjoy it, you'll become good at it. When opportunity knocks, open the door. Especially while you are young and have relatively little to lose, take an educated chance. Let one experience or phase in your life be the building block for the next. Keep moving ahead. You don't necessarily have to go to the most prestigious schools or work for the most prestigious companies or live in the big cities to become successful. It really is about you, what you are willing to learn, how you are willing to live your life, and how you treat other people that will make you successful.

It was during my tenure at Bi-Tech that I really came to understand the importance of working together with a really great team of people. If you have not already, you might take the time to read *Good to Great* by Jim Collins. In his book he talks about getting the "*right people on the bus.*" At Bi-Tech, Gary and Judy certainly had a knack for achieving this. There was a great sense that we were working with Gary and Judy, not just working for them.

Even in the early days of my time there, when the management structure was basically Gary, Judy, then everyone else, there was a sense of pride and purpose in what we were building. As the company grew, and certainly once SunGard acquired Bi-Tech, the management structure became broader. But even so, silos did not spring up. Silos are where a manager may think he or she can go it alone, doesn't need to communicate with the other managers, and runs his or her area without regard to other managers or the company as a whole.

***Lesson: Silos can be deadly to a company.***

Communication is vital among the managers and to the rank and file. It keeps everyone headed in the same direction. It lets you identify problems earlier rather than later and makes for longer-lasting relationships. Just like marriage. Make no mistake about this, though: everyone may have input, but ultimately the owner of the company has the final vote.

***Lesson: A company's management structure is not a democracy.***

You are going to meet many of the people I had the pleasure of working with at Bi-Tech and still enjoy as part of my life. I hope you get an appreciation of how talented these people are and can use this experience to help you instill some of these traits in yourself. Certainly you should look for these traits in people you may someday want to hire for your own company.

## Budgeting and Forecasting

Now a few words on budgeting and forecasting: for a young company starting out, just like a young family, it is very important to accurately budget your expenses against your revenue. When first starting out, this may really be more of a cash-flow projection, since cash is usually tight and, after all, cash is the stuff with which employees and overhead are paid. It must be realistic on the revenue side and cautious on the expense side. Too often budgets or forecasts are sprinkled with "a miracle happens here" scenario. Looking at your cash position, budget, and forecast may be an almost daily routine. You'll have to ask Gary sometime about his pullout board in his desk where he kept his cash and short- and long-term AR balances. He looked at it every day. Don't be afraid to adjust when reality is different from what you budgeted.

***Lesson: Don't rely or count on miracles.***

As the company becomes more sophisticated, budgeting will take on a different meaning. It will be what you measure your success against and what you publish to outside third parties. "Hitting your numbers" becomes much more important. Proving, over time, that you can accurately predict/budget how your company will perform will add to your creditability and therefore the value of the company.

Budgeting needs to be a team effort. All departments need to contribute to the process. Not just the sales manager, but other managers need to contribute what their costs will be at certain sales levels. Remember communication from before? If the manager providing customer support does not know the sales budget is to add a hundred new customers, how can he or she plan and cost out that level of support?

Ultimately it is the CEO/owner and CFO who vet out the budget. Sales always tend to be optimistic, except when setting their own quota, and managers always want to hire more people. All this has to be tempered to what can realistically be achieved. Looking at historical trends is always a good place to start, taking into consideration current market trends, new products, and competition.

***Lesson: Budgeting and forecasting are a team effort.***

When it comes to comparing actual results to budget, positive surprises are always better than negative surprises. In my CFO role, I always tried to create pockets of expenses in the budget. These were areas where we had some discretionary spending. In the event sales did not perform as budgeted, then I could draw on these pockets to reduce expenses, trying to maintain the same budgeted bottom line. Remember that in business, almost nothing goes according to plan. You always have to have room to maneuver. If the very worst happens, you have to be prepared to make difficult decisions to save the company. This may include a hiring freeze or perhaps an RIF—reduction in force. Or, as they say in the United Kingdom, redundancy. In the United Kingdom, it is very difficult to just fire someone. You need to show that his or her position has become redundant. In some of the acquisitions we did, we sometimes found many redundant positions.

***Lesson: In business, almost nothing goes according to plan.***

## Acquisitions

Speaking of acquisitions, I'd like to spend a few minutes relating some experiences about that. I'll defer to Gary and Judy about the decision process to sell the company. What I'd like to describe to you is more of the process of doing the acquisition.

The process performed by the acquiring entity is called *due diligence*.

Due diligence is performed by a team of individuals. There is the M&A executive who oversees and coordinates the entire process, and then there are various teams that look at all aspects of the acquisition target. These are accounting, finance, legal, HR, environmental, technical, clear title to the product, and others as necessary.

Due diligence is the process of pulling back the covers and looking deeply into every aspect of the target. Once the target is acquired, the acquiring entity takes on all the baggage, good and bad. You don't want to find out afterward that there are ghosts in the closet. From an accounting aspect, we were vetting the financials and projections. Did they make sense; was there a verifiable basis for the results and forecasts presented? Did the projections represent a "hockey stick (___/)?" Were they according to GAAP? If they needed to be adjusted to be in compliance with GAAP, what was the impact on the financials and the all-important *revenue recognition*?

***Lesson: Revenue recognition policy is critical.***

In the world of GAAP for software, just because someone pays you a license and maintenance fee, it does not necessarily mean you can count it as revenue. It may be deferred or spread over time depending on many variables. If we were acquiring a company that had not been following these GAAP rules, we needed to reset their revenue projections to fit these rules. Sometimes we would get a very bad answer; sometimes it worked in our favor. The worst answer would be that the revenue was never going to be recognized.

We would require the target to produce a tremendous amount of information. We generally requested every customer contract they had, and we read and summarized every one of them. We were looking for terms in the contract that could change the way the contract was accounted for or perhaps expose us to some liability or recourse in the future. Usually the target's owners did not want very many people at the target to know they were looking to be acquired. So we often worked off-site, but nearby. I worked for weeks one time from the basement of a law firm in London. When we did go on-site, we were often passed off as bankers or auditors.

I believe some of the best outcomes from our due diligence were in the companies that we did not acquire. Some were just not as they were being presented from a financial or some other aspect. I remember one company we looked at in Liverpool that had these great projections based on some software that was still being developed and had zero acceptance in the marketplace. Revenue recognition would have been deferred indefinitely. We decided not to take that one on.

Besides just looking at the projections of income and profitability, we also looked at the health of the target. Generally, by looking at the balance sheet over time, you can get a good sense for the health of the company and how the owner treated it. For instance, if there was low cash on hand, high AR, and high AP and other debt, it was being highly leveraged. Remember that when a company is acquired, generally the debt is a subtraction from the price paid. There is much less goodwill in a highly leveraged company than one that is not.

Being highly leveraged could mean the owner was not good at managing the company assets or was draining the company of necessary capital. Taking a look at the equity section of the balance sheet can reveal if excessive draws had perhaps been taken or there was never any capital invested. Either of these can be read that something is just not right with the way the company's assets are being managed. This situation would cause us to look much more closely in other areas to make sure they were actually as presented.

***Lesson: The balance sheet, over time, can show the health of the company.***

A balance sheet that is not highly leveraged, where owner draws are in line with earnings and where capital was being retained, showed us a healthy company picture. We were more inclined to be interested in such a company. So really, my message to you about mergers and acquisitions is that they can be a very arduous, time-consuming, and expensive process; you must be well-prepared with financial statements that can be verified.

**Lesson: Be well-prepared for an acquisition.**

A better meaning is you may fetch a higher premium for your company if it is well-organized and easy to vet and understand. One way to do this is to get a good accounting person (controller, CFO, whatever the title) on board earlier rather than later. The more "clean" history you can show, the more convincing your projections and forecasts will be. You should realize that any company you create needs to have an endgame in mind. Whether that is merger or acquisition or passing down in the family, start preparing for the event from the very beginning, even if you don't know what it is going to be. You do this by having a clean, well-organized, well-maintained, verifiable (auditable) accounting system in place. By system I don't mean the accounting software package, but the entire process, with people and documented procedures and practices, very transparent.

## Selected Axioms

Gary will present you with his twenty-two "Business Axioms." You should take them all to heart. If you can follow them, you should be a very successful business owner. I'm going to embellish on just a few of them from my own accounting perspective.

#5: Never borrow money. I, too, am a very debt-adverse person. It is critical that you never carry a balance on a credit card. However, depending on the type of business you have, you may need to take advantage of various financing vehicles available to you. One type is called asset-based lending. This type of lending is most common with companies that have inventory and accounts receivable that don't turn over very fast. Basically the company pledges as collateral the inventory and AR, and the lender will advance at a rate based on the value of the assets. An 80 percent advance rate on AR and 50 percent on inventory is fairly standard. There are, of course, conditions attached.

***Lesson: Never, ever, carry over a balance on a credit card.***

The lender is in first position if any assets need to be liquidated. They nearly always insist on a personal guarantee, so your personal assets go down with the ship if it comes to that. They insist on frequent collateral audits and constant refresh of the AR and inventory values. If the lender is a bank, it will certainly insist upon handling your treasury functions and insist that you use a lockbox for all receipts. What this means is they control your cash inflow, not you. Every penny that comes in first goes to pay the line of credit (LOC). To provide all this information, you'll need a good accounting professional and a good accounting system.

***Lesson: Depending on your business, you may want to use asset-based lending.***

#6: Don't confuse being smart with having a knack for something. Remember my statement earlier: I had found what I was good at and enjoyed and stuck with it.

#16: The best committee size is one. Did you know a camel is just a horse built by committee? Think about it.

#17: Get paid for your work. Your work has value; don't cheapen it by giving it away. Ask yourself, "Am I getting paid for this?"

#20: Don't let attorneys tell you how to run your business. I'll add accountants to this as well. Both are great resources, and you need both. But it is your company, not theirs. You need to make the decisions that are in the best interest of your company.

Bruce did an excellent job presenting to the students. Not only did he share some very important life lessons, he clearly depicted the role of the CFO.

# Business Realities: 59 Slides in 110 Minutes

Mark Fitzpatrick

Mark received his BS in computer science from CSU, Chico, in 1985. He is currently cofounder, CEO, and managing partner of FitzForm; and cofounder and CEO, YOUnite, Inc. He was a systems engineer with Data General from 1984 to 1988, joined Sun Microsystems in 1988, and worked there to 1993. He then spent one year as senior marketing engineer for NeXT. During the 1992 to 1993 time frame, Mark was the founder of Tidalwave Technologies (Firstwatch). From 1995 to 2000, he was the senior staff engineer for Veritas Software, a publicly held company with over 10,000 employees. From 2000 to 2013, he has been the youth director of Saint Matthew Archdiocese of San Francisco.

Mark believes his new venture, FitzForm, might be the beginning of the end of the drudgery surrounding the filling out of paper forms. His other company, YOUnite, holds patents on distributed patent sharing; Fitzpatrick says to think of it as a way to enable sharing of your Facebook profile without storing the data on Facebook servers. In his spare time, Mark teaches Catholic confirmation classes; he calls this his hardest job.

Mark and I share the honor of being designated "Distinguished Alumni" of the College of Engineering, Computer Science and Construction Management at CSU, Chico. However, that is not the reason I selected him. His vast experience and entrepreneurial drive made him perfect for the class. Mark holds the record for guest lecturers, ripping through 59 PowerPoint slides in 110 minutes and setting a pace that left the students spellbound. Most of this chapter draws directly from his slides.

Mark begins by telling the students that winners can handle setbacks, are willing to take chances, possess good instincts, and have some luck. He cautioned, "There are no guarantees." He then presents a very interesting definition of the three levels of happiness: selfish desires, accomplishment, and helping others.

## Technical

You should focus on application security and IT securing, and get a grip on white-hat hacking. There are a lot of good books and videos on white-hat hacking. If you are going to start a technology company, you had better get a firm grip on how hackers can take down your website and penetrate your web application and database servers. White-hat, gray-hat, and black-hat hacking are all the same thing, but from different perspectives. White-hat hackers are people blessed by the company to try to find vulnerabilities; gray-hat hackers find vulnerabilities, unsolicited, and let a company know there is vulnerability; and black-hat hackers are the mean people who enjoy or somehow feel justified in ruining other people's day. There are a lot of tools out there, from firewalls to intrusion-detection systems (IDSs), to help make sites and web applications secure.

***Lesson: There are a lot of bored, angry, smart people with massive amounts of computing horsepower at their fingertips.***

Having a good design upfront will save you *huge* in the end. Engineer a compatible look among your website, marketing literature, Facebook and LinkedIn, mobile applications, and web applications. As your company grows, appoint a creative director. Among this person's duties will be selecting fonts and colors that are consistent and pleasing. See www.kuler.adobe.com; it's a nifty utility for helping you find matching and complementary colors. There are plenty of others that help you pick nice flat web colors too.

***Lesson: People are visual and generally pretty impatient when it comes to software.***

Video → Try it → Buy it. Most people like games and tools, and the trend is that they really like them on their phones. Adults are spending about eleven hours a day either on their computer or phone. If you build something that provides recreation or utility, people will use it; however, it must be engaging. This starts from word of mouth, online app stores, social sites, or a website. The website may have a nice short video or animation or engaging graphics that have a call to action for the user. This call to action invites the user to sign up or download the app. This, in turn, gets the user to pay for the app or service. There may be a way to capture data or aggregate data that can be sold so the app or service can remain free.

***Lesson: For most products, people like to be sold if you have value and you make the process fun and engaging.***

Appoint someone to digital marketing. Ignoring it can be costly; starting it and then ignoring it is even more costly.

***Lesson: Leveraging the appropriate social-media platforms for your space can pay huge dividends and doesn't take a massive amount of work or money.***

The modern web-application software stack is comprised of:

- HTML/CSS/JS (runs in user's browser) or REST API consumer
- Web application
  - Handles requests for:
    - HTML/CSS/JS
    - REST API
  - Business Logic

  - o Backend beans that map to underlying data store; for example, MySQL or Mongo DB
- DB

***Lesson: If you don't get comfortable with the cloud, chances are you won't get far.***

It is imperative that a software startup have expertise in these things and know how to best implement them in the cloud. A big part of it is architecting the web application and DB servers so they can scale horizontally—that is, you don't scale by provisioning larger systems in the cloud, but instead, by provisioning more low-cost systems. Also, learn how to roll out new releases of software on a cluster of servers and how to do open-heart surgery on the data store.

***Lesson: Your software can kill somebody.***

- **Laser Story**: Mark shared a sixty-minute story where a medical laser device had a bug that was exposed when the technician entered the magnitude of the beam. If the technician made an error and backspaced, the proper value was displayed but the actual value was not changed. So people were getting zapped x10 or x100. It actually put holes in people.
- **St. Louis Children's Hospital ICU**: One of Mark's first sales of high-availability software was for the ICU at St. Louis Children's Hospital. Mark, recalling the laser story, went out and hired a guy who went on to be a world-class tester shortly thereafter.

***Lesson: Most startups don't put enough thought and resources into support; some recover and some don't.***

## Product Development Methodologies

Mark doesn't get too hung up on software design processes. He has seen controlling types abuse them, and by adhering to them too strictly, they destroy products and the spirit of a well-oiled team. They can become the tail wagging the dog; for example, someone holds up a release that customers are screaming for because some phase in the software development process wasn't done as agreed upon, even though everyone knows that the phase in question was insignificant or unnecessary for the given project. Mark asserts, "A scary sight is seeing a vocal yet minor contributor carrying around a software development process book, since you know that some future meeting is going to get hijacked into outer space over software methodologies."

That being said, Mark does list three methodologies and their intent:

1. MVP (minimum viable product) is good for prototyping and getting feedback.
2. Agile is often the preferred methodology for web applications that are on a rapid-release cycle.
3. Waterfall methodology is generally good for big releases, like shrink-wrapped software products.

Mark cautions, "Try not to get very deep on these things because it all comes down to figuring a process that will work for your customers and your company. When the company idea begins, do what it takes to get the features in place to create your core-value proposition. After that, you will need to get a sound software practice in place (Agile, Waterfall, or whatever works)."

Mark notes that for the web, Agile is probably the best practice—that is, short sprints that consist of well-defined requirements that aren't altered. If alterations are needed, then they can get pushed to the next sprint. The idea is that a rapid-sprint cycle is just as important as the features. So the developers create exactly what the sprint calls for, and once it is unit-tested, the source code is snapped, and the release is pushed to a testing server. Once it passes QA, the source is snapped again if needed, and pushed out to production.

- Product definition → integration testing → productization … what is your plan to carry it through?
- Productization is what it takes to make a technology marketable, sellable, usable, and supportable.
- What is the difference between a manager at In-N-Out vs. a professional group? A manager at In-N-Out is just there to make sure everyone is getting their job done and to step in as soon as someone is failing in his or her responsibilities. A professional manager is there to provide the resources the professional needs to get his or her job done, and only if there is a pattern of failing to deliver does he or she step in and begin to take corrective action. So philosophically, the In-N-Out manager's primary function is to monitor, and the primary function of a professional manager is to provide support.

***Lesson: Lots of people can build software, but few can productize.***

Mark poses some important questions:

1. Do I have developers looking for code nirvana? If they are, expect serious delays to market.
2. Who are my engineers? What are their skill sets? What types of projects are best suited for them?
3. Do I have marketers looking for product nirvana? If they are, expect serious delays to market.
4. Do I have project and product managers that still think they are working at In-N-Out? To make the point, Mark gives an extreme example: "Do I have a control-freak project manager who looks at his or her job as completely controlling how every aspect of the process is to work and tries to squeeze every last ounce of energy from the developers and dictate how things are to be done? Or do I have a project manager who looks at himself or herself as a resource to help the developers get their job done better? Another point worth mentioning: Are my business, sales, and product

managers trying to tell the engineers how to get things done? The businesspeople need to stay in their lane, as the developers need to stay in theirs."

### Offshore Development

Developers in India are around $3,000/month, Argentina $4,000/month vs. California at $10,000/month++ (total cost). You must spec things out very clearly and dialogue daily (Skype). Your goal is to have your specs ready one project or two ahead of the developers. With offshore development, it is possible to have a twenty-four-hour development cycle.

> ***Lesson: Hiring developers in California is very, very expensive; great developers can be found overseas if you clearly specify what you want.***

### Tools

Mark provides a list of tools that have helped him in his development efforts.

- Google Docs
- Dropbox
- Skype
- Photoshop/Illustrator
- HTML
- Projectors
- Mobile WIFI
- Password Manager
- Balsamiq
- Wiki (any)
- GitHub
- Pingdom
- Jira (the dashboard)
- Whiteboards
- Video Conf (webex)

### Business

Completing the technical part of his presentation, Mark launches into the business development part of a startup. Business development finds the initial business opportunities. The connections they establish are *huge*, as are the channels they establish. Once sales references and channels are in place, then you develop sales. Mark referred to this phase as "Coin Ops." He also shared that resellers can be fantastic; give them exclusives for big bucks.

Mark next dives into what makes for good salespeople. He tells the students to "develop one-minute, three-minute, and full product pitches; if you don't, you're toast." Salespeople are generally more honest than engineers; remember the trusted advisor from Drake Brown's chapter (chapter 2). He goes on to state that good salespeople have a reduced fear of rejection, and the real good ones are either calm and articulate or mad dogs on rock-cocaine.

You probably have something that someone else needs and for which they will be thankful. People generally will listen to your one-minute pitch. Your disposition should be that you don't want to waste your time or theirs if it looks like there isn't a fit. If there isn't a fit, ask for advice on what would make it a good fit, or if there is anyone they know of who might be interested. Can they tee-up an intro? Good listeners do better than talkers; remember Drake Brown's chapter. If there is a fit, bite down hard and don't let go.

Mark recounts an interesting story for the students; names have been changed. "Bill was a new-hire rep at the VS computer company, and he closed his first big deal. It was a new account called XYZ Company. The purchasing agent at XYZ had to convince some of his cohorts to go with VS. Finally, the purchasing agent told Bill the PO was ready late in the afternoon, and Bill was so happy the deal finally closed, he figured he would go out and play some hoops and have a few beers to celebrate, then pick up the PO in the morning. Unfortunately, that night, the purchasing agent passed away of a massive heart attack, and the other players in XYZ cancelled the PO. So, as soon as you have a chance, close the deal, get the signatures, and then run far and run fast, since there are plenty of stories of how partying with the client after a deal closed has exploded too."

Mark touches on trade shows. Beginning with the assertion that most people will give you one minute to make a pitch, Mark went through a possible trade-show booth dialogue.

You: "Can I bug you for just one minute?"
Them: "Sure, okay, just one minute."
You: "Hi, my name is Biff," extending your hand.
Them: "Hi, my name is Bob," shaking your hand.
You: "Nice to meet you." (Launch into your one-minute pitch.)

***Lesson: Most trade shows are cheesy, but they can net huge dividends.***

## Company

Mark presents a segment on the formation of the company. He starts by telling the students that friends and relationships you make now can yield real-life events down the road. He speaks to the type of company you can form.

1. sole proprietorship
2. partnership
3. limited liability corporation (LLC)
4. S-corp

Mark has only seen LLCs and S-corps get real funding. LLCs lack a board of directors and generally are easier to operate. LLCs pass their earnings on to the owners every year, whereas S-corps can retain them.

If you have no money, what can you give away to attract talent? Equity, but you only have one hundred points. Stock options (S-corp). Lofty job titles. Board seats on an S-corp. Advisor positions for an LLC. Hefty sales percentages for early business development work.

Mark shares an instructional horror story on stock options. Stock options are tricky *so talk to your accountant; all tax disclaimers apply.* Stock options aren't taxable until you exercise them (or at least at the time of this writing; the laws may have changed recently); but once you do, there is a tax event. I don't have the exact numbers, but I heard of this happening multiple times:

- Catherine got 1,000,000 stock options at 0.10 a share and the stock was trading at $30.10.
- She paid or borrowed $100,000 to exercise her 1,000,000 options at .10 a share and was now sitting on $30,100,000 of stock.
- Her friend told her to hang onto the stock, since if you hold it for a year, it becomes a long-term gain and the tax rate is lower.
- The stock price starts to tank.
- Catherine waits for the stock to rebound, but it never does and the stock is worth next to nothing.
- Tax time comes, and the IRS says she purchased $30,100,000 worth of stock for only $100,000, so she owes tax on a $30,000,000 gain. Even if it is long-term, she owes around $10,000,000 in taxes.
- Pain ... misery.
- She goes to the IRS for a reduction. They are real nice to her and give her coffee, but say "sorry." She still owes them $10,000,000.

Mark concludes his unit on stock options with the following: "Bottom line: as soon as you exercise stock options, see a conservative accountant and sell enough stock to make sure you can pay your tax bill. And my added neophyte investor advice: sell enough so that you don't feel like a moron if it goes to zero, but at the same time, have X that says, 'If it hits X, I'll never need anymore, and I will cash out.' And I'd add, have a laddered approach to how you can trim the stock tree; work with a professional advisor on this. More advice: I don't work on my car anymore when it breaks, and I don't handle my money. I found that accountants and money managers have more than paid for themselves. Your job is to find accountants and money managers that you can trust."

***Lesson: Understand the risks of stock options.***

Mark gives good advice on the use of attorneys. They help with corporate formation, draft sales and employment agreements, draft partnership agreements, and draft nondisclosure agreements (NDAs). Mark cautions the students to avoid the big firms while you are small, even if they will work for free. They generally aren't truly working for free; but rather, they will simply defer the bills, and you end up with massive liability down the road. They will even grab your funding when it comes in. You can find attorneys who will work for equity.

On the subject of patents, Mark points out that they are expensive; some VCs like them and others don't care; don't bother with international patents. He also says, "Accept that trolls will be your friends." The press, in large part, due to their friends at large corporations, have painted trolls as evil. Trolls are companies, usually staffed by patent attorneys, that don't create technology, but either acquire patents or represent companies that hold patents. The misconception that trolls clog the courts with frivolous cases isn't true, since if a firm shows a pattern of this, it runs the risk of contempt-of-court charges.

If you are a small company and hold a patent that a large entity is violating, there is really nothing you can do unless you have a large war chest with which to litigate. The large entities will merely ignore all your letters informing them that they are violating your patent. To make matters worse, the large companies that used the standing patent laws to gain their position in the world are trying to change them to benefit their own interest and weaken the standing of small companies.

If you have a patent that is being violated by an entity, understand that you would only go after a company if it is damaging you—that is, collecting revenue in a space where you tried to make money. Then, your only recourse as a small company is to either (1) get a big war chest and throw the dice on litigation using a firm that knows the ins and outs of patent courts, or (2) hand your patents over to a troll who will probably split the proceeds with you once they subtract out their costs. They often charge nothing unless they win or settle out of court. Also, they don't take just any patent, but only if they are well-written and have truly novel claims that are, in their minds, being violated by profitable entities.

The odds that someone is going to stop what they are doing and chase your idea are remote, at best. Of course, most funding sources are very happy to sign NDAs. However, don't share your idea with someone you don't know well who is closely connected to a company that could easily integrate your idea with their existing product.

***Lesson: Don't be paranoid about sharing your idea.***

## Funding

For funding, Mark says you have four choices.

1. **Friends and Family (FnF)**: If you haven't alienated the people near and dear to you and they want to see you succeed, this is the easiest way to raise money.

***Lesson: Never take money from FnF unless you warn them that they may never, ever, see the money again. If you don't succeed, there will always be a white elephant in the room with your ex-investors.***

2. **Crowd Sourcing**: You need to completely expose your idea to get funding.
3. **Seed and Angel Funding**: Try to find angels who have existing connections in the space you are trying to penetrate or, even better, will be your first customer.
4. **VC Funding**: You need to show how you are getting customers and converting them to dollars. You need to show how their money is going to transform your company to reach more customers and extract more money from the customers, and in turn, make them fabulously rich(er). Many do have huge war chests and are under the gun to find places to invest. Many *don't* want to make small investments. Will their investment help you? John Doerr (venture capitalist) says, "No conflict, no interest." In other words, "If I can't wire the investment to succeed through my existing connections, with other companies and entities, then I'm not going to fund it." Traunching: when a VC invests in you with the designs to increase your valuation (good). They work into the deal that in the following round of funding (now that you are more valuable), they will get all of their money back (bad),

and then they will essentially have their equity for free. You will need all of the money to grow.

***Lesson: Most VCs have great connections; unless you have real traction or an amazing track record, you aren't going to get VC funding.***

## Truly Important Stuff

Mark concludes his outstanding lecture by giving advice to the students and listing some books he likes.

**Sleep and Rest**: Get all that you can, but be ready for all-nighters. Try not to work when you are very unproductive. Mark tries to take all of Sunday off. His Mondays and Tuesdays are much more productive when he does.

**Help**: People don't like to give help, but they do love to give advice. Your network of contacts can be as important as your product. *Get on LinkedIn* and start building your network today.

***Lesson: Always ask for advice and never ask for help.***

**Sixth Sense**: Mark offers this interesting observation to the students. "We have our five senses (vision, hearing, touch, smell, and taste), but just because we can't put some under a microscope doesn't mean we don't have more. At the highest level, there is an obvious sixth sense of *spirit*. We can get a sense of good and bad spirit by our daily interaction with people. You see a kid bullying another and feel the bad spirit or energy; or you see a granddaughter hugging a grandmother and feel the good spirit.

"By virtue of wanting to do a good job in computer science, we often become so focused that we are like zombies; it's as if our friend could be on fire across the room and we wouldn't even notice. As computer science professionals, we need to recognize this, and step back at times and make a conscience effort to unplug and be human. An easy first step is to reach out to someone who you know would love to hear from you, not someone you want to hear you. There is a big difference. The boy or girl you have a crush on is probably not the candidate, but the friend you have who is struggling with a relationship probably is. We are geeks and we like to quantify things; measure this in smiles per hour. Did you put a smile on someone's face? You just got to the positives of the sixth sense, and it gets you back into being a human."

***Lesson: Being human is a good thing.***

**Study**: The general pattern to learning technology for an entrepreneur or leader is summary (friends, YouTube, Google, etc.), dabble, more study, then spec out and hand off or become a master. Understand how to communicate effectively, read and lead people, and deal with adversity. Develop these traits with a passion equal or greater to your passion about technology. Without a moral compass, much of this is impossible to do well.

Mark concludes his chapter by listing his favorite books and movies:

Movie, *American Graffiti* (early George Lucas)
Movie, *Local Hero*
*Home Computer Revolution*, by Ted Nelson
*The 22 Immutable Laws of Marketing*, by Al Ries and Jack Trout
*The Civil War*, by Ken Burns
History Channel's *The Men Who Built America*

*Your list will be different.*
All we really want is to be truly happy.

That concludes Mark's chapter. It was a challenge for the students to keep up with him; however, they loved his presentation.

# 8

# Global Sourcing and Startup Funding: When You Come to a Fork in the Road, Take It

Daren Otten

Daren Otten is currently the vice chair of the department of mechanical engineering, mechatronic engineering, and sustainable manufacturing at California State University, Chico.

Within industry, Daren worked both domestically and abroad in contract manufacturing, providing engineering, manufacturing, and project management support to companies, such as HP, GM, Hamilton Beach, Jacuzzi Brothers, and Epson. Previously, he served as the interim CEO of a startup green plastic company in San Diego, codirector of the North State Innovation Lab, and president of a product development and contract manufacturing firm based in Northern California.

He also currently serves on the advisory boards of Butte College/Butte County Office of Education ROP Welding CAD/CAM, & Manufacturing Programs; Sierra College/Lincoln High School District IDesign Program; Butte College Drafting; Butte College Business; and is also part of the executive and board management teams for Innovate North State, North Valley Learn, and the Work Training Center.

Daren has a BS in industrial technology/manufacturing management and an MS in manufacturing engineering; and during this semester, he successfully defended his doctoral dissertation at CSU, Sacramento. I got to know Daren while I was working on two patent projects. Each involved extruded plastic components, and Daren owned a company that was able to build prototypes. Only one of the projects ended up getting a utility patent, but in the process, I got to know Daren quite well. It helps that we both love to duck hunt and we enjoy the occasional fine cigar.

When I decided to offer the class, I selected Daren to do two lectures. Mainly because he has extensive experience in global manufacturing and sourcing, venture pitching, project management, and startup success. He also gives sage advice on startup failures.

In his opening comments to the class, Daren said, "When you come to a fork in the road, take it." While this is clearly a Yogi Berra quote, it conveys to the students that action is what makes things happen. The lesson also is reflective of being flexible to opportunities and customer needs. Customers will ultimately tell you if what you are doing is valuable and provide insight into what could or would be valuable. The trick is to maintain core competencies of the organization while being flexible to opportunity.

## Project Management

After giving the students a brief background discussion, Daren launches into the very important topic of project management. He begins by describing the four phases of project management.

1. **Initiate**: This is the startup phase, which occurs before budgets are set and scope is defined.
2. **Define and Organize**: In this phase we develop the project goal, definition, scope, and requirements.
3. **Track and Manage**: There are four major components in this phase, where all the "real" work is done. The components are planning and resource allocation, track and control, reporting, and review. In these components we find scope management, work-plan management, resource management (cost, time, and people), deliverable management, quality management, transition plan, and internal/external vendor management.
4. **Close**: This is where we complete the project and provide an assessment of our success in meeting the stated goal.

Each project comes with risks. **Technical Risks**: The technology developed or employed may not meet the requirements, or work at all. **Schedule Risks**: The project tasks may take much longer than planned. **Resource Risks**: The existing budget or personnel may not be adequate to complete all the project tasks.

***Lesson: Know the risks of a project and have a backup plan.***

## Global Sourcing

The decision to go global requires very careful consideration. Daren gives the students a few examples. Firestorm, a Northern California wildland contract fire-suppression company developed some unique safety products. Based upon a market research study, the manufacturing price point was critical. The products have relatively complex components, with multiple parts and assembly required. The assembly contained custom manufactured plastic components, circuit boards, light-emitting diodes (LEDs), switches, battery mounts, and lenses. The multitude of components required significant assembly, and the total production volume was low enough that automation of this assembly was not feasible within the economic constraints of the project.

Balancing the costs of the parts, quality, and cost associated with assembly is generally a numbers or quantity game. The higher production volume of the given widget offsets the cost associated with automating the process for assembly. With low production-volume components that require significant assembly, it is almost impossible to not rely on human labor for this task. And lower labor costs, relatively speaking, can be found in many areas outside of the United States.

***Lesson: Lower labor costs can be found outside the United States.***

Daren then passes around a small container from Rapid Ramen Cooker. Rapid Ramen is a startup company that is beginning to experience growth. Price is a critical item, but a combination of price and terms drove the deal. Asian manufacturers tend to be willing to negotiate in this area. For a startup company, cash flow is often the biggest challenge. Creatively negotiating terms with vendors can help manage some of the swings associated with the production of product. In most vendor/supplier relationships, the startup company, which has limited if any established credit, often must pay 50 percent of the cost of custom tooling. Typically, six to ten weeks later, the balance of 50 percent is due with approval of first-article parts.

This cost can be significant, with Daren having been involved in projects that ranged from very low to well over one million dollars in these costs, which must be absorbed prior to any revenue being generated by the custom tooling. After the first articles, production and assembly time can range, depending on volume and supply-chain constraints, from a couple of days to months. After production, the products must be shipped. If the product is being transported via ship container, ocean time is roughly two weeks, customs is often a week, and truck transport from port to the startup facility can be another week. Thus, it takes approximately thirty days to get the parts to the ordering company's domestic facility.

For most companies with thirty-day terms, payment for these goods would be due about the time the products are received, once again forcing an outlay of cash without the requisite inflow. Many foreign manufacturers are willing to negotiate on these terms, providing sixty- to ninety-day terms, which can hopefully help balance cash flow a bit better for the startup. It does not hurt to ask all potential contract manufacturers, both domestic and abroad, about extended terms when selecting and qualifying a vendor. Daren found many Asian suppliers more flexible regarding finance terms.

***Lesson: Try to negotiate payment terms more favorable than thirty days.***

Daren cautions the students that the wage gap is reducing between the United States and much of Asia. Lenovo, a Beijing-based computer maker, opened a new manufacturing line in Whitsett, North Carolina, to handle assembly of PCs, tablets, workstations, and servers. While it's still cheaper to build things in China, those famously low Chinese wages have risen in recent years. "We reached the point where we could offset a portion of those labor costs by saving on logistics," NA (North America) President Jay Parker says. Lenovo was able to justify producing the goods in the United States for two main reasons. One, their volume is significant enough to justify the automation of much of their production; and two, producing goods near or within markets significantly reduces transportation costs.

***Lesson: The wage gap between the United States and offshore is decreasing.***

Daren specifically points out that one of the largest challenges is the ability to predict transportation costs very far forward due to swings in fuel costs. Often it is difficult to pass these fluctuating costs onto consumers, so minimizing transportation costs as much as possible hedges this volatility. The other part of this equation is a product's susceptibility to transport damage and relative size. Big-screen televisions are expensive to ship and can be fragile.

***Lesson: Reducing the transportation distance of completed products limits exposure to damage and reduces transportation cost.***

It makes sense for international container-load shipping where thousands of products can be shipped with minimal damage concerns. However, when only a couple of items can fit within a container or are fragile, higher production costs that involve less transportation are often justifiable. It is critical to look at the total production cost of a product, which includes transportation time and expense, along with packaging, insurance, and tariffs.

***Lesson: It is critical to look at the total production costs of a product.***

Daren also cautions the students to be aware of currency exchange rates. "Currency exchanges throughout the world are still extremely volatile. With the dollar not as strong as the yen, our customers are anticipating a price advantage on machines manufactured here, since import costs will be eliminated," according to Mark Mohr, president of Mori Seiki, USA.

***Lesson: Currency exchange rates are volatile.***

For producers of consumer widgets, be it televisions, computers, or cookware, currency-exchange fluctuations can change the economics of production. Within the United States, a drop in the value of the dollar as related to the yen, for example, reduces the purchasing power to the domestic consumer. However, this same devaluation makes it less expensive to manufacture products within the United States for global companies.

These windows are often short-lived as monetary policy generally attempts to minimize deflation or inflation adjustments. But this can prove to be an economic advantage to the company that is savvy about where goods are produced and sold. This same fluctuation can provide opportunity and danger associated with previously mentioned supplier financial terms, which may have been negotiated under more certain economic conditions. As the entrepreneur, you may have done a great job negotiating terms with your global suppliers, but still get pinched when your retailers are paying you 90 to 120 days after you have delivered product.

## Startups and Raising Money

Daren encourages the students when doing startups to give careful consideration to five aspects of the company.

1. **Structure**: Don't just think of the initial structure of your startup; give thought to how it will be organized after growth.

2. **Intellectual Property**: How are you going to protect that which makes your product or service unique?
3. **Protection Strategies**: How, as the principal, can you protect yourself and your assets?
4. **Resources**: Where will you get the needed funds to get your business going and growing?
5. **Exit Strategies**: Keep this in mind when you read Michael Reale (chapter 9) on this topic.

Daren approaches the funding issues by giving the students some excellent places to look. Daren playfully refers to the primary source to look at for seed financial resources as the AT&T plan. The AT&T plan refers to one's friends and family. These people are the most likely source to turn to for initial investors into a startup. These dollars are often committed with just faith in you and a hope that the venture is one that is successful and they will be rewarded in some fashion.

Most early family investors structure these as loans or convertible notes. In the case of convertible notes, the advantage is that the seed-stage investors have their investment valued at a later stage, often when later-round money, such as angel or venture, is being added to the company. This postsecondary money increases the value of the investment upon conversion and overcomes the challenges of valuing an early seed-stage company.

***Lesson: Friends and family are often the first source for funding.***

**Government Cheese**: Two programs specifically allow for small business to pursue government funding supporting research and development of products in which various government funding agencies have an interest or need. The Small Business Innovation Research (SBIR) and Small Business Technology Transfer (STTR) multiphase grant programs end in a scale commercialization to meet the needs of the government and possibly other industries. While it is a very competitive process to ultimately be successful with the grants, it should not be overlooked as both a seed for ideas and a resource possibility for the entrepreneurial company. There are many great technologies within the STTR realm that are looking for industrial partners to scale and commercialize. Daren gives three references to the students:

- SBIR/STTR
- www.zyn.com
- www.sbir.gov

The SBIR program is a highly competitive program that encourages domestic small businesses to engage in federal research/research and development (R/R & D) that has the potential for commercialization. Through a competitive awards-based program, SBIR enables small businesses to explore their technological potential and provides the incentive to profit from its commercialization. By including qualified small businesses in the nation's R & D arena, high-tech innovation is stimulated and the United States gains entrepreneurial spirit as it meets its specific research and development needs.

The STTR is another program that expands funding opportunities in the federal innovation research and development (R & D) arena. Central to the program is the expansion of the public and private sector partnership to include joint-venture opportunities for small businesses and nonprofit research institutions. The unique feature of the STTR program is the requirement for small business to formally collaborate with a research institution in Phase I and Phase II. STTR's most important role is to bridge the gap between performance of basic science and commercialization of resulting innovations.

***Lesson: Don't overlook the government as an initial funding source.***

The SBIR Program is structured in three phases:

***Phase I.*** The objective of Phase I is to establish the technical merit, feasibility, and commercial potential of the proposed R/R & D efforts. The objective is also to determine the quality of performance of the small business awardee's organization prior to providing further federal support in Phase II. SBIR Phase I awards normally do not exceed $150,000 total cost for six months.

***Phase II***. The objective of Phase II is to continue the R/R & D efforts initiated in Phase I. Funding is based on the results achieved in Phase I and the scientific and technical merit and commercial potential of the project proposed in Phase II. Only Phase I awardees are eligible for a Phase II award. SBIR Phase II awards normally do not exceed $1,000,000 total costs for two years.

***Phase III***. The objective of Phase III, where appropriate, is for the small business to pursue commercialization objectives resulting from the Phase I and II R/R & D activities. The SBIR program does not fund Phase III. For some federal agencies, Phase III may involve follow-on non-SBIR-funded R & D or production contracts for products, processes, or services intended for use by the US government.

There are other places to turn to for funding as well. While not always conventional and popular, sources, rules, and regulations are constantly changing, and crowdfunding such as Kickstarter has proven to be a popular place to both promote and fundraise. Private companies within the contract manufacturing space are also getting into the seed-stage funding game. Kick2Real is a program just launched in March 2014 by Foxconn as an attempt to diversify the products that they manufacture. Finally, there are always reality television shows, such as *Shark Tank*. The Rapid Ramen product Daren mentioned before was successful in obtaining resources from Mark Cuban through the reality television show.

Daren provides links to these alternative options:

- http://kick2real.com/
- http://kickstarter.com/
- http://abc.go.com/shows/shark-tank/video/PL5539712

***Lesson: There are alternative funding options.***

## Accredited Investors vs. Unaccredited Investors

Wherever you obtain the funding required to get your startup going, there are a few things that you should be aware of when soliciting investors. Daren highlights the difference between accredited and unaccredited investors. He stresses that once you are past friends and family money (and even with them), it is best to involve the services of a business attorney with significant experience in raising money and issuing stock and ownership to investors. There are limits on the number of unaccredited investors a company may have and significant rules about solicitation for private equity offerings.

Rule 506 of Regulation D is considered a "safe harbor" for the private offering exemption of Section 4(2) of the Securities Act. Companies using the Rule 506 exemption can raise an unlimited amount of money. See http://www.sec.gov/answers/rule506.htm for details.

Daren follows his discussion of seed-level investors by describing the difference between angels and venture capitalists. Angels tend to be the first funding entity to a startup after friends and family seed money; venture capitalists tend to come in after the startup has a financial track record. Generally speaking, investors of any type want to see customers, sales, and revenue. The company might be operating at a loss, but the marketplace has expressed interest in the products or services. This interest can provide a bit of insight into the possibilities of scaling the operation. This provides significant comfort for investors.

Daren speaks at length about the Band of Angels, to whom he has pitched, although he has never successfully closed a deal with them. They are highlighted as they are one of the groups that most startups know about and immediately turn to. They were formed in 1994, have 127 members, and meet monthly to review the top three deals. Since 1994, 209 deals have been done; $186 million has been invested, forty-five of the companies have been profitable, nine went on to an IPO, and over 3,000 jobs have been created. The Band of Angels has a very diverse portfolio, with a high-tech focus. Members of their portfolio include Internet/web services, software, network/telecom, life science/biotech, semiconductor, and electronics and industrial.

The Band of Angels funded eleven new startups in the past twelve months, along with five follow-on investments. The average capital provided was $275,000. The average amount of time to close financing after the presentation is six weeks; the longest was 7.5 months. In the past twelve months, 697 deals were submitted; ninety-two companies met with the deal-screening committees; thirty-four were selected for presentations, and eleven received funding. Daren cautions that big-time angel groups, such as the Band of Angels, will not often be bankrolling multimillion-dollar finance requirements.

***Lesson: The Band of Angels awaits your proposal.***

## Startup Success and Startup Failure

If the customers don't like your idea, try something new. If they like part of the idea, develop that. And if it fails, keep trying until you succeed. Know when to fold 'em, know when to hold 'em. Your customers are your best bet in identifying areas of need that will provide value to them. They will vote with their wallets on what they will pay for. Often, as you develop your business or product, only one very small part is what will ultimately be successful. You must manage your pride and ego, and approach solutions with an open mind. Your customers will judge your output and reward you accordingly.

**Manage and leverage debt.** As a startup you will likely not have the luxury of unlimited resources, and generally you will be required to sign personal guarantees for any loans or credit that you need for your business. Often these loans also need to be collateralized. Sometimes this can be done with company assets or receivables, but often banks want you to pledge more. Do your best to avoid pledging your primary residence. Having almost lost a house that he used as collateral during a challenging business cycle, Daren asserts it can take one's focus rightfully off the business when it is needed the most. This is an added stress that, if possible, one should avoid.

***Lesson: Avoid stressful leveraged debt.***

With personal guarantees that are uncollateralized, ensure during ownership changes, such as the sale of the business, or business-structure adjustments, such as sole proprietorship to an S-corp, that legally binding documents are created that assign this personal liability to the new entity. If after selling a business where the new ownership assumed debt, and then defaults, it can be disastrous when the lender comes back to you, often years after the sale was completed.

***Lesson: When acquired or restructured, make sure personal liability is assigned to the new entity.***

**Consider structure change as debt/leverage climbs.** Often startups are originally formed as sole proprietorships, partnerships, or S-corporations. The structure that worked well when the organization was started may not always work well as potential liability increases. These liabilities are not always related to debt. As always, consult with your attorney, but creative company structuring and restructuring can provide layers of security to the founders regarding debt, product liability, investors, and other potential sources of litigation.

Long-term product liability is another reason for structure changes. If the products that your company makes have any potential liability regarding human life or limb, such as is often found with medical, automotive, or safety equipment, structures that isolate the company founders from personal litigation are critical. Often it is liability mitigation that drives the multiple holding companies, subcorporations, and stand-alone divisions that are found in many organizations.

***Lesson: To mitigate liability, restructure as you grow.***

**Going back to the "well."** Often entrepreneurs will need to raise more capital than originally planned. This can happen during seed-stage, angel, or even venture rounds. Often the best folks to go to are those who have already invested in you. They already have an interest in seeing you succeed, and as long as you are continuing toward a goal that they still believe you may achieve, these are your best sources for more resources. These follow-on investments are generally made with new terms and valuations, and can often pinch the company owners, as follow-on investments never want to squash or dilute previous equity.

This often leaves the founding group in a place where control may become a concern and must be managed delicately. When your current investors say no to requests for additional resources and they have the capacity for additional investment, you must truly look at your plan objectively. When investors say no, they are often looking at their previous investment with you as lost and additional funds would be good money chasing bad money. This should always act as a wake-up call when the "well" runs dry.

***Lesson: A dry funding well is a red flag.***

**Personal liability/bankruptcy.** Silicon Valley is full of successful entrepreneurs, and almost every one of them has failed in some business venture. The goal is to manage the liability and minimize the impact on your nonwork life. This failure is never fun while going through it nor will it be fun to discuss in the future, but as they say in life, if you learn from it you will be better off.

Bankruptcy laws in the United States ultimately protect the entrepreneur. As long as the business failure was not a criminal or an intentional act of fraud, you will not end up in jail. You will receive many harassing phone calls, which you will refer to your attorney, but you will be able to move forward onto the next chapter. Hopefully that chapter will include another foray into the world of startups, as these protections exist to support the risk takers and the job creators, and foster those who challenge the world with new ideas. Will you be proud of your failure? Not likely, but should it prevent you from trying again? *Never*!

**Lesson: Bankruptcy, while painful, need not be fatal.**

**Constantly revisit the exit strategy.** Daren shares the pinch points that many entrepreneurs come to as a business gains a level of success. This success builds a comfortable place for founders and key employees and is often referred to as a lifestyle business. The lifestyle that is afforded by the business gets principals thinking about family legacy, and at some point this approach can squelch the ability for risk and opportunity taking. If the goal from the outset was to create a lifestyle business, great; mission accomplished. Even then, however, this is not the time to rest. Succession planning and ownership issues must continue to evolve.

Many entrepreneurs look at the dream of being acquired or sold, which is not a lifestyle business. The acquisition time for these companies is when financial reward can be realized. Depending on the speed in which a business evolves, exit plans need to be reviewed annually, sometimes quarterly, to ensure that the business decisions still align with the exit plans of the founders. It is possible that you can move between a lifestyle or acquisition-based business, but one must always keep the endgame in mind.

**Lesson: Your exit strategy should be reviewed annually or quarterly.**

It is easy to understand why Daren has been honored as "Instructor of the Year" by his students. His two class presentations were filled with valuable and insightful information for the aspiring entrepreneur.

9

# Finding Opportunity: It Helps to Look Like Tom Cruise

Michael Reale

Michael has been married to Janine for twenty-plus years and has two daughters, Alex (age fourteen) and McKenna (age twelve). In addition to sounding and looking like Tom Cruise, Michael has a very interesting background as an entrepreneur. He graduated with a business degree from Cal Poly, San Luis Obispo, a very prestigious institution. From 1995 to 1998, Michael was a consultant with Deloitte & Touche, a huge international consulting and accounting firm. Michael helped with the implementation of large and complex accounting systems. That's how we came to know him; he was helping a client who had selected IFAS.

In 1998, Drake Brown, our marketing and sales VP, contacted Michael to offer him a position as regional sales manager at Bi-Tech after they met working on a joint proposal with Deloitte & Touche. The position caught Michael's attention because he desired to learn more about the mechanics of a software company, as he had aspirations of starting one of his own at some point in his career. Michael took the job because it let him do the entire sales cycle, from initial contact, RFP preparation, demo scheduling, and closing, through contract negotiations. Michael is an amazing young man who did great work during his tenure at Bi-Tech.

One of the most significant aspects of Michael's success at Bi-Tech was his ability to become a "Trusted Advisor" to prospective clients. Michael saw this as having three phases: vendor, credible source, and trusted advisor. Of course, I will never forgive him for leaving and stealing two of our best software engineers!

From 1994 to 1995, Michael worked for the Sacramento Blood Center as an account manager. This involved multiple people keeping manual schedules for blood drives; then these people would come together to schedule the resources needed to support the blood drives in a central schedule. All this manual work left much room for error. Michael knew there could be a better way. He knew what the software needed to do, he knew there was no competing package available, and he knew he would need programmers to create the package. In the late nineties, when Michael joined Bi-Tech, he was able to identify the programmers he would need.

***Lesson: Always look for a better way to do something.***

Michael's career as an entrepreneur was launched because he paid attention while working for a blood bank in the mid-nineties. In 2001, Michael founded and became president/CEO of Altivation Software. Its primary product was Hemasphere, a CRM/event management/staff scheduling software package that services the blood-banking industry and automated the manual task of blood-drive scheduling and account management. (CRM is an acronym for "customer relationship management.)

The first few years were a struggle as Michael and Janine self-funded the startup of Altivation Software; however, in time, the package gained considerable traction. After eight years of steady growth, Altivation had a 93 percent market share, with 100 percent of the American Red Cross banks. Clearly a "blue ocean," as you will soon learn more about. His company was acquired by Haemonetics, Inc., a publicly traded medical-device company, in 2009. Following the acquisition, Michael stayed on with Haemonetics for approximately eighteen months, where he oversaw the research and development of the blood-banking software division.

Michael is also the cofounder of Run for Food, along with his wife, Janine. Run for Food was started in 2006 and is a 5K event to raise money for the Jesus Center, the local food bank and homeless shelter in Chico. In 2013, it completed its eighth annual run. The event now has over 5,000 participants, generates nearly $100,000 in net proceeds, and has seventy-five corporate sponsors and 215 volunteers. In their experience with Run for Food and other races, the Reales got to know the mechanics of putting on a race. They also observed that the organizational process was tedious and manual (sound familiar?).

***Lesson: Giving back to the community can become profitable.***

In 2011, Michael founded and became president/CEO of Exit Row Solutions. The primary product is RacePlanner.com, a CRM/event registration software product that services the race/training program industry. The genesis of the name of his current company is interesting. The commercial flights out of Chico are on a puddle-jumper airline called United Express. Seasoned travelers know to ask for the exit row because it has more legroom and you can get some work done during the short flight to San Francisco. The company was dreamed up while Michael sat in the exit row. Exit Row Solutions has experienced significant growth. In 2013, it signed a national agreement with Girls on the Run International, a curriculum-based after-school program for girls in grades three to eight. The company experienced a 500 percent increase in revenue from FY2012 to FY2013.

I can't wait to see what Michael's next innovation will be. He's still young and not nearly ready to retire. He made an interesting comment to my class. He said he remembers sitting in an airport with me and asking if I had any thoughts on selling Bi-Tech. I said, "I wish I had done a better job of planning an exit strategy." Michael said that stuck with him, and he always starts a company with an exit strategy in mind. This makes a difference because how you plan to exit your company may change the way you manage and grow it.

## Entrepreneur Defined

Topics Michael covers include the following: Do you have what it takes to do a startup? Can you wear more than one hat during a startup? Are you uniquely qualified to succeed in your startup? How do you differentiate your product/service for success? Which business model is best for you?

He begins by listing what you need to do with your startup.

1. Start it (fund it/resource it).
2. Build it.
3. Test it.
4. Market it/sell it.
5. Implement it.
6. Support it.

Michael tackles the definition of an entrepreneur. He quotes Tom Post in an article from Forbes.com that states (in honor of Startup Month at Forbes.com in February 2012), "It's time to make an important distinction about what a true entrepreneur is. The reason? Because it concerns the very engine of economic growth and the people we desperately need to rev it up."

Consider two definitions of *entrepreneur.* Merriam-Webster: "One who organizes, manages, and assumes the risks of a business or enterprise." Dictionary.com: "A person who organizes and manages *any* enterprise, especially a business, usually with considerable initiative and risk."

The difference is subtle, but fundamental: it's the word *any.* Dictionary.com has it right: entrepreneurs, in the purest sense, are those who identify need, *any need,* and fill it. It's a primordial urge, independent of product, service, industry, or market. It is also interesting to note that this definition makes no reference to revenue.

***Lesson: People can exhibit the entrepreneurial spirit in any endeavor they adopt, revenue-seeking or not.***

The US economy needs all kinds of entrepreneurs, from coders to clockmakers, in order to close its widening fiscal hole. *But the relentless, seek-and-solve breed is our salvation.* They are the ones forever craning their necks, addicted to "looking around corners" and "changing the world."

They, not lenders, are the real money multipliers—the ones who turn $1 of capital into $2, then $2 into $10, and $10 into $100.

This is the true essence of entrepreneurship: define, invest, build, and repeat. "It's just balls-out fun," crowed Steve Spoonamore, serial entrepreneur and founder of ABSMaterials, a member of Forbes's list of America's Most Promising Companies. "There are people who love to sail the ocean or climb mountains, and more power to them—but it's nowhere near as interesting as taking a technology nobody has heard of, finding a market for it and launching it to your customers. That's satisfying." (from Forbes, 2012)

***Lesson: Few things in life are more fun than owning your own company.***

## Uniquely Qualified and Startup Stress

Michael's remarkable success is the direct result of him being "uniquely qualified." His experience with blood banks gave rise to his first enterprise. His experience with races gave rise to his second enterprise. Michael poses three important questions to the students.

1. What in your *past* experience makes you uniquely qualified to start a technology company?
2. What in your *current* situation makes you uniquely qualified to start a technology company?
3. What do you see in your *future* that uniquely qualifies you to start a technology company?

**Uniquely**: Being the only one of its kind.

**Qualified**: Having the abilities, qualities, attributes, and so on, necessary to perform a particular job or task.

***Lesson: Before starting your startup, make sure you are uniquely qualified.***

Michael tells the students about stress and the startup. Starting a technology company is not a stress-free endeavor. He begins by giving them an Internet reference to a TED talk by Kelly McGonigal on how to make stress your friend: http://www.ted.com/talks/kelly_mcgonigal.

He asserts that the most powerful lesson from her talk was her closing comments, where she stated, "Chasing meaning is better for your health than trying to avoid discomfort. Go after what it is that creates meaning in your life and then trust yourself to handle the stress that follows."

## Red Oceans, Blue Oceans, and Business Models

Michael indicates that reading and learning from other entrepreneurs is very important to growing professionally once you launch your startup. One book that strongly impacted Michael was *Blue Ocean Strategy* by W. Chan Kim and Renee Mauborgne. This book helps entrepreneurs find a niche in the market and separate themselves from other competitors they may face. Two market segments are defined as red oceans and blue oceans. From the book, Michael offered the following definitions:

> "**Red Oceans**: Industry boundaries are defined and accepted, and the competitive rules of the game are known. Companies try to outperform their rivals to grab a greater share of existing demand. The space is crowded, profit and growth are reduced. Products become commodities and cutthroat competition turns the red ocean bloody.
>
> "**Blue Oceans**: Untapped market space, demand creation, and the opportunity for highly profitable growth. Most blue oceans are created from within red oceans by expanding existing industry boundaries. In blue oceans, competition is irrelevant because the rules of the game are waiting to be set." (Boston, MA: Harvard Business Press, 2005, 4–5)

While Michael was working at Bi-Tech, a red-ocean enterprise, he came up with the idea for a blue-ocean enterprise, Altivation Software. He encourages the students to start working for large firms that swim in the red ocean, but to continue to give serious thought and dreams to creating a blue-ocean enterprise.

***Lesson: Red oceans are good places to think about blue oceans.***

Michael concludes his presentation by asking the students what type of business model would be appropriate for their entrepreneurial aspirations. Specifically in the world of technology, some of the choices are:

- **Traditional**: Selling a product or service where someone pays you outright for your product or your service one time.
- **Transactional**: Revenue generated from a transaction where someone pays you each time he or she uses your product or service.
- **Subscription**: Revenue generated from subscriptions to your product or service, where you receive a monthly/annual subscription fee for the use of the software, regardless of how frequently the product is used.
- **Other**: Noting that "one size fits all" does not apply to a business model, possibly take from each of the models to build one unique to your product or service.

Based on the number of student questions and comments after his presentations, I would say Michael hit it out of the park. Thank you, Michael.

# 10

## International Commerce: From the Big Top to the World

Jessee Allread

Jessee Allread secured international business relationships into and out of the United States with Australia, Canada, China, Czechoslovakia, France, Hong Kong, India, Israel, Japan, New Zealand, Singapore, Sweden, Switzerland, and the United Kingdom. He created international trade agreements and operations in these countries with strategic relationships, product distribution, manufacturing, and fundraising. Given that many of the students will go on to compete internationally, I felt Jessee was just the right person to set their expectations and help them understand, at a detailed level, how to navigate international commerce. Jessee's slides, notes, and edits were used by me to write this chapter.

Jessee worked for Toys R Us, Autodesk, Starpath, and eBook as startups and many more startups as a consultant. He is currently working with two startups: a United States-based work-truck supply chain and a mobile game company.

Jessee's family owns and operates Grace Jr., a local gift store celebrating its fiftieth year in business. (Nearly half of Judy's presents come from Grace Jr.!) Jessee is a close personal friend who has a most unusual childhood background, perhaps explaining his lust for travel: Jessee grew up with parents who owned a circus.

Jessee begins his lecture by imploring the students to engage in detailed research before entering the international arena.

*Lesson: Research is the key to international entrepreneurial efforts.*

## Research, Research, Research!

The key to entering international business involves dedicated research into the prospective foreign market. Understand and have a plan to deal with the time-zone differences and language differences. Know the rules of entry: visas, import/export, and ownership. Identify any prohibitive regulations or restrictions. Are you looking for direct sales or indirect? Some trusted research sources Jessee recommends using are:

1. US government
2. Universities
3. Chambers of Commerce
4. Civic organizations
5. Business organizations
6. Friends and family
7. Prior business relationships
8. LinkedIn

You must also research the competition. Is there any? What's your target market and why? Who's the market leader? Why are they leaders: first to market, insurmountable barriers to entry, defensible intellectual property? What are their weak points, and who are their competitors? What is the TAM (total addressable market) and SAM (share of addressable market)? Can you get money out of the country? How volatile is the monetary exchange rate? Can you partner with a trusted person living in the country and familiar with local customs? Are you going to increase market share, or take it from an existing market participant? Have you considered the travel costs?

A good rule of thumb for reselling a product or service is 50 percent of the stated price. With products, that's half of MSRP (manufacturer's suggested retail price). Supply-chain pricing varies with the method in which you sell. If you're selling direct to the consumer, you'd better automate all of your ordering and fulfillment processes. If you sell through a retailer, you need to support that link in the chain with incentives: samples, giveaways, advertising, co-ops, and the like. Selling through a distributor is typically a volume play, and an offer of a 60/40 split to reach your target customer is not unreasonable. Always review competitors' pricing and market norms to ensure your goods or services can be sold at a profit long-term.

While we were running Bi-Tech, we developed a product that would automatically convert systems from a proprietary platform to a UNIX platform. We called it TRANSPORT. We ended up with some international interest in the product and developed distributors in France, Germany, England, Spain, Denmark, and Mexico. We made just enough money off the product to make a couple of trips a year to visit with our distributors. It was fascinating how differently business is conducted in each of these countries. Probably the most interesting country was England. We would spend eight hours in a long, ponderous meeting, accomplishing nothing, then go to the pub and get work done.

***Lesson: Every country has a different way of doing business.***

## Access and Introduction

When considering a foreign country, you must develop a strategy for access and introduction. Begin by developing your market-entry methodology. There are several avenues in which you can enter an international market. You may have an affinity for a particular marketplace. There may be a trade event that targets your demographic. You may have received a purchase inquiry from a credible buyer. Perhaps you're looking for close proximity, such as the United States, Canada, and Mexico. In the case of your specific product, a market fit may be obvious: an emerging market segment promoted by your target country's government.

***Lesson: Access and introductions are key elements in international business.***

Jessee prefers two primary methods of initial market research: trade shows and purchase inquiries. Each is an inexpensive method to begin your review of an opportunity. Trade shows require little more than ensuring that the attendees or exhibitors fit your business. Are you selling direct or through distribution? Are the exhibitors displaying products or services complementary or competitively to yours?

Are the attendees prospective buyers or resellers of your product or service? Note: There are times when researching new sales opportunities, you will find a market segment others have not yet entered. Attending such a trade event may allow you to be first to enter this new market opportunity, one your competitors have overlooked. Here are a few examples: 1) cloud computing in the midst of increased hard-drive capacity, 2) mobile communication in areas where no landlines exist, and 3) micro loans in third-world countries.

***Lesson: Be on the lookout for new market segments.***

Purchase inquiries may be gold or gold-painted lead. You will certainly pay attention to an individual or organization wanting to purchase your product or service. Communication with such an inquiry can be quite revealing. Responding to such an inquiry should be done with some amount of caution, though. Are they interested in buying your product, or are they researching your company? Introductions to new markets can come from every source available to you. Communicate your interest to your network, review the responses, and act accordingly.

Review the various sources of information available for the trade event or purchase/reseller opportunity. Once you decide to attend a trade event, you begin by seeking appointments with your purchase inquiry or preferred supply-chain prospect: consumer, retailer, distributor, licensor, or OEM (original equipment manufacturer). Never attend a trade show without set or scheduled appointments with those you are considering involving in your business.

***Lesson: Never attend a trade show without set or scheduled appointments.***

You must start with those you trust and can verify; be sure you do reference checks. I'm sure you've all heard of the phrase "six degrees of separation," the theory that everyone and everything is six or fewer steps away, by way of introduction, from any other person in the world. Just look at Facebook or LinkedIn to understand how those you know can introduce you to those you want to know. Jessee prefers to reduce that number to three degrees and poses a theory that after years of a dedicated career, you should be able to reach anyone you wish with a single contact. Whether or not that individual responds to you depends upon the quality of your connection.

***Lesson: Facebook and LinkedIn can help with introductions.***

## Partnership, Production, Distribution

For in-country distribution, consider developing a contractual relationship with a native. Be cautious with the working of this contract and take the time and money to engage the services of an attorney experienced in international agreements. How are you going to deliver your product or service? How will your product or service reach its customer safely, with the smallest number of links in the supply chain? How will you handle defects and returns?

***Lesson: Have an attorney draw up the contract with an in-country representative.***

Every country has some variation of a distribution supply chain. After overcoming the language barrier and after you're certain that you understand how the supply chain works, the simplest method of conducting business in any country is to sell your product or service paid-in-advance until you have developed a trusting relationship. Obviously there are exceptions to every rule. An example would be a clearly identified leader in distribution that demands terms, marketing, advertising, technical support, and some form of in-country presence. Leading organizations can demand this and more.

Depending upon the popularity and acceptance of what you're selling and the depth of your pocketbook, you may be able to choose among several options:

1. Contact a US distribution firm to determine whether or not they have an overseas presence. Ingram Micro is one such US distribution company that operates in most foreign countries.
2. Select the largest retailer (bricks and mortar, online, or both) and contact them directly.
3. Attend a trade show that has supply-chain participants exhibiting and attending, learning who best fits your model.

All reputable distributors and retailers prefer you have multiple products to offer their customers. Offering multiple products or services reduces distribution risk. Consumers are fickle; they return stuff, claiming defects when there is nothing wrong with whatever they're returning. The supply chain is sophisticated enough to allow returns and, in fact, enable immediate returns without question as their best method of customer service and to keep the consumer dollar, already spent, in their pocket, not their competitors'.

Credit for a return is common practice, and if you don't have a second product to exchange, you are a riskier distribution partner. Multiple products or services give comfort to the supply chain that you will be able to satisfy a broader audience and a dissatisfied customer with an exchange of product, not a return of the dollars they've already collected.

***Lesson: Plan for product exchanges.***

A defective product does require exchange. Most supply-chain components will be able to share what percentage of inventory they require to satisfy exchange instances. Defective exchanges are rarely returned up the supply chain. When they are, they're destroyed, not returned to you for exchange. Include this in your COGS (cost of goods sold) calculation.

As you may imagine, having a robust engine for returning or crediting funds from all types of transactions is a basic requirement. What will be your access or reporting from such a system?

When developing any supply-chain relationship, always consider each component of an end-to-end transaction. Consider sourcing components to construct your product, including packaging, which may not be returned with the product. Also consider shipping, handling and delivery costs, training, support, instruction guides, demonstration, samples, spiffs, bribes, and other moral dilemmas you might face. A spiff is generally a manufacturer-based incentive, for example, a bonus, an immediate cash reward, or an increased commission offered to a salesman to move a particular product.

## Banking, Legal, IP (Intellectual Property), and Security

Every country you choose to do business with has rules that vary from those of the United States. Yes, there are treaties that provide some protection, but have your team of professionals advise you in advance of entering into any agreement or relationship. Such preparation will save you losses in the future.

***Lesson: Learn the business rules of your target country.***

Your local banker may be able to introduce you to a bank he or she does business with internationally. Your attorney, CPA, or trademark professional will be able to ensure that you have choices in each country you plan on entering. If not, change professionals.

There is a pair of very simple rules you should follow without consulting anyone:

1. Don't ship, download, or provide anything before you're paid.
2. Don't sell into a market if your intellectual property has not been protected.

One source for reviewing international sale contract law is the UN Convention on Contracts for the International Sale of Goods, CISG. http://www.cisg.law.pace.edu/cisg/biblio/perovic.html#iia. As in all things business, have your attorneys review and advise you on specifics, always try to be paid in advance of shipment, and ensure through research and references that you are dealing with reputable people and organizations.

## Wrap-Up

Jessee recommends that the students read Gladwell's *David and Goliath* and *Tipping Point*. He also suggests they visit www.santiva.net. In addition to your average Internet search to secure travel, trade-show, or translations services, here are a few sources Jessee always uses:

Trade Event Links
http://trade.gov/
http://www.tsnn.com/
http://fita.org/conferences.html
http://export.gov/%5C/tradeevents/index.asp

Travel Links
https://travel.americanexpress.com/travel/home
www.kayak.com/

Visa/Embassy Links
http://travel.state.gov/content/passports/english/country.html
http://www.projectvisa.com/

Purchasing from or selling into a foreign country is exciting. You can find bargains for your business on either side of the transaction.

Jessee knows of individuals who have visited countries to buy or sell goods and have never had a problem. He also knows of piracy, theft, and failure. Whenever you can mitigate risk by consulting those who have gone before you, do so.

Jessee's class presentation was extremely informative and very appropriate. Over half of the students in the class are foreign students, many of whom plan to return to their native countries to begin a business.

# 11

## Project Management: Everything's a Project

Sean Morgan

With over three hundred complex implementation projects, Bi-Tech learned the true value of good project management. Many of our implementations took well over one year to complete. Coordinating the activities of people not in our employ was the most daunting aspect of our projects. I ran into this challenge very early in my career. One summer, a year after Judy and I were married, I got a summer job with Alpha Beta Acme Markets in Southern California. I was to write an assembly-language fleet-optimization system for dispatching trucks. There was one key person in the installation, Elsie, who was beyond resistant to change. I tried every way I could to get her to buy in, but to no avail. Finally I went to my boss, Bill Cowan, and told him the problem I was having. He walked out of his office, leaned over Elsie, and said something. He came back into his office and told me I would not be having any more issues with Elsie; I didn't. When I asked Bill what he had said, he replied, "I told Elsie if she wanted to come to work Monday, she would have to get on board with the new system." The point here is that effective project management is well-served by strong managers who can incent buy-in.

When I decided to teach this class, I wanted the students to get a comprehensive presentation on project management. Whether they go to work for a company or do their own technical startup, they will be very well-served to understand the vital role project management will have in their success. In a 2011 survey of companies conducted by Panaya/SAP, the respondents listed the skills most important to securing higher pay. Project management was first, with 51 percent, followed by analytical, with 39 percent.

Given the great importance of this topic, I had to select someone who walked the walk and talked the talk. That turned out to be quite easy—Sean Morgan. Sean teaches a wildly popular 400-level course on project management, and he has all the appropriate credentials—plus he' a successful entrepreneur. His students call him "Captain Morgan."

Academically, Sean has BS degrees in finance and international business from Chico State. In addition, he holds an MBA from Chico State, a Project and Strategy Management Certification from Stanford, and a Business Dynamics Certification from MIT.

Sean started his first company while still an undergraduate at Chico State. After twelve years as a business owner, he returned to Chico State for his master's degree and started his second company, Legacy Business Concepts. Today Sean teaches project and strategy management for Chico State's College of Business, continues to run Legacy Business Concepts, and is the managing partner of a small consulting firm.

Sean ran in a crowded field for Chico City Council in 2012 and won a seat on the council. While his multiple hats keep him busy, his primary love is for his wife and two boys, Ashton age fourteen, and Zachary age twelve, who are both avid athletes competing in football, basketball, and martial arts. Sean and I first met because Ashton and my grandson Max play on the same basketball and football teams. I liked Sean from the start. Although he's sort of a politician, he doesn't worry much about being politically correct; and we both share a fairly conservative view of government. I could be described as a little to the right of Louis XIV.

Before presenting his two lectures, Sean gives the students two reading assignments. The first related to a Pentagon contract in the range of thirty to forty billion. The air force had been trying to replace its fleet of KC-135 air-refueling tankers, the big jets that act as flying gas stations for warplanes. In the latest attempt, three companies wanted to submit bids to build the KC-X, the next generation of tankers: Boeing, EADS, and US Aerospace. Each company's bid was required to be submitted to an office at Wright-Patterson Air Force Base in Dayton, Ohio, by 2:00 p.m. July 9. US Aerospace's bid was five minutes late, and thus was not considered.

***Lesson: If you're going to submit a bid, be on time.***

The second reading assignment was a fifteen-page report on the Hubble telescope mirror project. It was written by Robert S. Capers and Eric Lipton and titled "Hubble Error: Time, Money, and Millionths of an Inch." In this excellent article, the authors demonstrate what can happen when project management runs amuck. The results were hundreds of millions over budget, many years of delayed delivery, and a flawed mirror launched in April 1990.

## Project Management

Sean begins his presentation of project management with a quote from Van Gogh: "Great things are not done by impulse, but by a series of small things brought together." Project management is the process of managing all the elements of a project. A project is a unique effort with a defined beginning, a defined end, a specific deliverable, and defined resources. Project management gets its roots from construction, engineering, and manufacturing; it is now integrated into business, management, finance, IT, and many other endeavors. The focus is on execution, and it fosters integration.

Today's companies must modify and introduce products constantly, respond to customers quickly, and maintain competitive cost and operating levels. The old wisdom was to compete by either low cost, product innovation, or a focus on customer service. The new wisdom is to focus on all of these aspects.

Project management takes place outside the normal, process-oriented world of the firm. Twenty percent of global product ($12 trillion/year) is spent on fixed capital projects worldwide. Trillions more are spent on projects involving IT, new products and services, entertainment, NGOs (nongovernmental organizations), and politics.

Vision without action is merely a dream. Action without vision just passes the time. Vision with action can change the world. The project management mantra is "On time and under budget!"

***Lesson: Project management is vision in action—that is, execution.***

Now that Sean has the students believing in the importance of project management and its basic precepts, he launches into certifications. He begins with one of the largest in the world, PMI (Project Management Institute). There are over half a million credential holders, 250 chapters, and twelve global standards. The PMI publishes the industry premier standard, *Project Management Body of Knowledge,* which boasts over three million copies in circulation. The processes described in the PMBOK are consistent with other management standards, such as ISO9000 and the Software Engineering Institute's CMMI. The guide recognizes forty-seven different processes that fall into ten knowledge areas: integration, scope, time, cost, quality, human resources, communication, risk, procurement, and stakeholder management.

The Certified Associate in Project Management (CAPM) is for project team managers and entry-level project managers, and undergraduate or graduate students with interest in project management. It requires 1,500 hours on a project team, or twenty-three hours of project management class instruction. Sean's MGMT 444 class counts. The student must pass a 150-question computer-based examination. Sean's final exam is designed to be more difficult than the PMI exam; for example, he has five multiple choices vs. four on the PMI exam.

The next level of certification is Project Management Professional (PMP). This requires 7,500 hours in project task leadership positions, sixty months of project management experience, and thirty-five hours of project management education. Other PMI certifications, Sean notes, include Program Management Professional (PgMP) and PMI Risk Management Professional (PMI-RMP). PgMP is for people responsible for multiple related projects within a program. PMI-RMP is for those who identify project risks and capitalize on opportunities. Sean also mentions the PMI Scheduling Professional (PMI-SP) certification for those concentrated in developing and maintaining project schedules. For the truly elite credential, there is the Stanford Advanced Project Management Certification (SCPM). There are only around four thousand certificate holders, among them, Sean.

Sean explains why there is so much interest in project management: there is a growing number of projects, current PMs are retiring, and not many academic programs are offered in project management; thus, there is a gap between supply and demand. The *Wall Street Journal* says students should gain skills, not just degrees. They must be effective communicators, analytical, team players, and technical, and possess a strong work ethic. Companies want employees who communicate effectively, think critically, solve problems and execute solutions, collaborate with teams in the office or across the planet, and can be creative without specific technical knowledge.

Sean concludes this part of his lecture on project management with some important points. PM degrees and credentials are transportable across functions, industries, and geography. The jobs will be there. The PM has entry into one of the fastest-growing professions. Of course, increased earning potential is compelling. In closing, he encouraged the students to visit www.pmi.org and to surf job sites for project jobs.

***Lesson: Certified project managers make more money than those uncertified.***

## Project Management in Action

Sean abandons the ten-thousand-foot level and drills way down into project management. All projects should have a goal, a project manager, organization, tasks to be performed (summary level and subtasks), and timing for tasks. All projects have resources, a budget, an end date, and conflicts (trade-offs).

Companies that increase predevelopment emphasis have increased successful new product commercialization by a 2–1 ratio. Winning projects spend more than twice as many resources on predevelopment activities. Changing requirements induce more delays in product development than any other cause.

***Lesson: Put the work in up front and avoid delays and budget overruns.***

Sean presents a more granular definition of a project: "A unique set of activities meant to produce a defined outcome within an established time frame using a specific allocation of resources." In your pre-project development, provide a project objective statement. Use plain, simple language, make it clear and concise, use twenty-five words or less, and provide vision. Sean gives the project objective statement for the moon shot: "Put a man on the moon and return him safely by December 31, 1969, at a cost of $9B."

The pre-project development must lay out the major deliverables. Define the project's outcome, resources needed, and focus of the project team. Your layout must be well-defined and clearly understood by all stakeholders. After your initial pre-project work, go on to the project framework. Here you will establish team attendance rules, participation guidelines, formal issues log, access to the project file, communication strategy, and conflict-resolution guidelines.

The next phase of the pre-project development is the work breakdown structure. Its main purposes are to echo the project objectives, present an organization chart for the project, create project logic, communicate project status, and improve project communication, control, and understanding. Key questions to be asked in the work breakdown structure formation are: Are all the tasks identified? Is project planning included? Are task times included? Do tasks have owners? Do lower-level tasks have only one owner?

When you are going about a task, you've got to think about the big things while you're doing the small things, so the small things go in the right direction. If pre-project development is done well, the battle is half over. Sean finishes with a quote from World War II General Eisenhower: "No battle was ever won according to plan, but no battle was ever won without one ... Plans are useless, but planning is indispensible."

By now, the reader of the preceding chapters has seen a consistent theme among the presenters. Sean did a great job of driving this concept home.

***Lesson: Planning before you act is extremely important.***

## Team Leadership vs. Management

Many of these students will go on to work in teams. Sean gives an excellent unit on team leadership and team management. What's the difference? Is one better than the other? Management is a function—planning, budgeting, evaluating, and facilitating. Leadership is a relationship—selecting talent, motivating, coaching, and building trust. Many team individuals take on the leader's goals, values, commitments, and personality.

Sean continues by listing the four management decision methods. First, there is **consensus**, where universal agreement is achieved. This is slow and steady. Martin Luther King Jr. wrote, "A genuine leader is not a searcher for consensus but a molder of consensus." Second, there is the **autocratic** method: "I say, you do." Third is the **consultative** method, where you strive for consensus, then you make the final decision alone. The fourth is the **manipulative** method, where you appear to be consultative but you really are autocratic.

How do teams make decisions—many times poorly? This is due to a lack of defined evidence, circumstances, time, and conflict. Conflict is a lack of agreement or harmony. It's a fight, battle, or war. It's a process resulting from tension among people due to real or perceived differences.

There is **affective** conflict, where we have an emotional disagreement characterized by anger or hostility. There is **task** conflict, with a content-focused disagreement over what is to be done. And there is **procedural** conflict, where there is process-focused disagreement over how something is to be done. Managing conflict in diverse teams requires the manager to listen, focus on the issues, not the person, focus on data (not opinions), get alternatives, and focus on the common team goal.

***Lesson: As the project manager, be prepared to deal with conflict.***

When I ran Bi-Tech, we typically had a Monday-morning meeting with all the employees. It was designed to cover a variety of topics, lasting less than thirty minutes. When we didn't have a major topic, I would roll out my standard "getting along" speech. I would explain, "We can come up with about the same number of reasons to like someone or not like someone. If you are working together, it will sure help this company if you choose to like each other."

## Class Project

Sean finished his second lecture with a riveting class assignment. He divided the class into teams of four people. Each team was tasked with answering many questions about the Hubble project. When the teams were about to start, Sean turned on some ear-bursting music—so loud that the team members had to write to each other to communicate. Next, he turned off the lights. After a few gasps, the students used their cell phones as flashlights and continued to work. Soon after, Sean came to each team and told them they had experienced a budget cut, and Sean sent one member from each team outside the classroom. It was a frantic twenty minutes, and the students, while a little rattled, loved the experience.

It was a very entertaining microcosm of teamwork. The students were able to experience working in a team with a very short time line, intervening variables, and unexpected circumstances. One of the students decided to add one more semester so he could take MGMT 444 from Sean.

Thus, we conclude the chapter on Captain Morgan. It is easy to see why students hold him in such high regard.

# 12

## Social Media and the Virtual Company: Keeping Bees and Clients

Mike Monroe

Mike is my nephew; thus, it's unlikely I'll say anything bad about him. I had the advantage of knowing Mike as he grew up and knew him to be supersmart. Before joining Bi-Tech, he was an apiculturist—fancy word for beekeeper. He was hired to do training and consulting on our various systems. He adapted very quickly, and our clients just loved working with Mike. In 2007, he became a very successful software demonstrator; please see appendix 1 for some notes I wrote up to help him demonstrate successfully—they'll help you too.

In 2009, Mike broke out on his own and became president and CEO of Koa Hills Consulting, a technology and management consulting firm. Koa Hills delivers exceptional professional services, including ERP implementations, business process reengineering, project management, managed services, financial software consulting, software training, strategic technology planning, and software development. Koa Hills focuses on local government, school districts, research organizations, and other nonprofit organizations.

Mike has successfully grown Koa Hills Consulting to include fourteen employees and many highly skilled third-party resources. Prior to founding Koa Hills, Mike spent twelve years serving as a software consultant for SunGard Bi-Tech, where he was one of the most sought-after consultants for IFAS core financial modules. His extensive experience as a software product consultant has positioned him to excel as a project manager as well. He has successfully managed a number of large-scale, complex software implementations, where he coupled his in-depth technical skills with structured project management.

In his role as president and CEO at Koa Hills, Mike is responsible for all company operations and final hiring decisions. He has attracted an incredible group of talented professionals who are extremely dedicated to Koa Hills and its clients. Under Mike's leadership, Koa Hills has developed a proven track record of delivering projects on time, on budget, and according to specification. Koa Hills is also a Google partner.

The main reason I selected Mike to be a guest lecturer in my class was not because of his impressive credentials; it's because he highly leverages social media to promote his company and runs his very successful company as a completely virtual entity. Mike likes living in Hawaii, and his employees are scattered throughout the United States. Many of my students may find they need to run a virtual business. Mike offers a road map on how this can be effectively done.

## Social Media to Promote Your Business

Mike begins with a definition of social media: "Conversations and sharing information through online channels." He traces the time line of social media from the postal service in Persia in 550BC to Twitter in 2006. He shows the monthly unique users of the top fifteen social media sites. Finally, he describes the top eight.

| | | |
|---|---|---|
| **Facebook** | 1 billion | Age demographic: 18–29 years |
| **Twitter** | 310 million | Age demographic: 18–29 years |
| **LinkedIn** | 250 million | Age demographic: 30–49 years |
| **Pinterest** | 150 million | Age demographic: 18–29 years |
| **Google+** | 120 million | Age demographic: 18–24 years |
| **Tumblr** | 110 million | Age demographic: 16–24 years |
| **Instagram** | 85 million | Age demographic: 18–29 years |
| **VK** | 80 million | Age demographic: 35–44 years |

| | |
|---|---|
| **Flickr** | 65 million |
| **MySpace** | 40 million |
| **Tagged** | 38 million |
| **Ask.fm** | 37 million |
| **Meetup** | 35 million |
| **Meetme** | 10.5 million |
| **Classmates** | 10 million |

**Facebook** is the leading social network, providing a popular free networking website that allows registered users to create profiles, upload photos and videos, send messages, and keep in touch with friends, family, and colleagues. The site, which is available in thirty-seven different languages, includes public features, such as:

Marketplace—members post, read, and respond to classified ads.
Groups—members with common interests find each other and interact.
Events—members publicize events, invite guests, and track attendees.
Pages—members create and promote a public page built around a topic.
Presence technology—members see which contacts are online and chat.

Facebook is an excellent place to promote your company; however, Mike warns, you need to be vigilant about monitoring it. Koa Hills uses Facebook for branding and marketing.

***Lesson: Don't ignore postings on your Facebook page.***

**Twitter** is the leader in microblogging, accommodating a community of people actively discussing everything from politics to food to fashion to technology. Mike's clients incorporate Twitter into their daily lives as a way to connect with their interests and discover useful information. It's a real-time conversation about what matters to each of us, brands and businesses included.

**LinkedIn** connects the world's professionals to make them more productive and successful, with access to people, jobs, news, updates, and insights that help them be great at what they do. Thirty-six percent of businesses say they use LinkedIn for various reasons, including engaging with others in their industry and extending awareness of their business. Koa Hills uses LinkedIn for recruiting, branding, and marketing.

**Pinterest** is a visual discovery tool that people use to collect ideas for their different projects and interests. People create and share collections (called "boards") of visual bookmarks (called "pins") that they use to do things like plan trips and projects, organize events, or save articles and recipes.

**Google+** is the second leading social media, providing a networking platform for discovering and sharing digital content with friends, family, and coworkers. It provides connectivity, usability, networking, video sharing, and conferences. Google Hangouts is widely used in Mike's company. He shows a wonderful example to the class by linking up with one of his employees in Virginia, demonstrating how they can each work on one document. Koa Hills uses Google+ for advertising, branding, marketing, and recruiting.

**Tumbler** is a microblogging platform and social networking website founded by David Karp and owned by Yahoo! Inc. The service allows users to post multimedia and other content to a short-form blog.

**Instagram** is a fun and quirky way to share your life with friends through a series of pictures. Snap a photo with your mobile phone; then, choose a filter to transform the image into a memory to keep around forever.

**VK** is the second largest social network in Europe (after Facebook), available in several languages. Like other social networks, VK allows users to message contacts publicly or privately, create groups, publish pages and events, share and tag images, audio, and video, and play browser-based games.

Mike states, "Your customers are already there, and you can meet them there for public relations, marketing, loyalty, thought leadership, customer service, collaboration, networking, lead generation, research, and recruitment."

***Lesson: Social media can be exploited to grow your business.***

Mike concludes his lecture on social media by providing some interesting data points and then gives the students his seven steps to productive business use of social media. In a 2011 American Express survey, 35 percent of the respondents used online social networking in their business.

Mike provides some other interesting metrics. Ninety percent of all purchases are subject to social influence. One-plus million sites have implemented Facebook's social layer. Thirty billion dollars is the predicted revenue for social commerce markets in 2015. Ninety percent of consumers trust recommendations from people they know. Groupon had $11 million in one-day sales for GAP. Pampers sold one thousand diapers in one hour on its Facebook store. Baby & Me show that 50 percent of their online sales come from Facebook.

Every company needs audiences to survive. They are where you find new customers and develop more profitable relationships. For businesses with limited resources, social media has been a blessing. The sheer number of tools available can be daunting.

***Lesson: Master social media; it's nearly free.***

The seven steps to productive business use of social media are:

1. Focus on desired outcomes first.
2. Incorporate brand personality and voice.
3. Identify the smallest segments possible of your audience.
4. Identify the communities for these micro-segments.
5. Identify the influencers of these communities. Mike quotes Jake McKee's 90-9-1 principle: 90 percent are audience, 9 percent are editors, and 1 percent are creators.
6. Create an action plan with metrics. Metrics include sales, increase in awareness (e.g., # Facebook ad views), product interest (e.g., #

of clicks, # of fans), conversion of new customers (e.g., # of online purchases), cost per lead, reach (audience growth rate), referral-site traffic, social product mentions, and "relational equity" (e.g., positive responses, feedback).

7. Interactively execute and measure results.

## A Virtual Reality

Mike sets his agenda to define a virtual company, list the benefits, establish a virtual company, and manage a virtual company. A virtual company by definition is "an organization that uses computer and telecommunications technologies. It extends its capabilities by working routinely with employees or consultants in various locations. It uses collaborative tools, such as e-mail, calendar sharing, chat, videoconferencing, and documents centrally stored and accessible from anywhere at any time. Virtual teams operate without the physical limitations of distance, time, and organizational boundaries. They use electronic collaboration technologies and other techniques to lower travel and facility costs, reduce project schedules, and improve decision-making time and communication."

The secret advantage of an entirely distributed company is that everyone uses the same tools to communicate. Everyone! From Boiney, 1998, "two-thirds of Fortune 1000 companies are using self-managed and virtual teams to reduce real-estate expense, increase productivity, generate higher profits, improve customer service, and access global markets."

***Lesson: Virtual teams = teams + electronic links + groupware.***

***Lesson: A virtual company has reduced overhead.***

In establishing a virtual company, Mike first advises, "Mind your strengths." Stick to what makes your company exceptional; outsource the rest. This will win business, generate good margins, and make you unique. Farm out any work for which you can't charge a premium, like bookkeeping, travel reservations, and server backups. Next, "Keep it real" by using technology to bridge the miles, and don't forget the human element. Next, "Leave little wiggle room" by being precise and clearly defining expectations. Then, "Treat resources like staffers" because the best contractors can always work for someone else; treat them well. Finally, "Don't be clueless" by having only one person understand the job.

Mike goes on to explain the four secrets to managing virtual employees.

1. **Set the ground rules**. Set the ground rules to ensure efficient employee performance. Employees should have a dedicated working space and hours; they are expected to be within reach of their phones or computers. Your company policy needs to be clearly stated so that employees are held accountable.
2. **Provide some face time.** For both the sanity of the employee and the manager, there needs to be some face time throughout the week, for example, Google Hangouts, webcams, Skype.
3. **Have adequate reporting**. As a virtual manager, you will not be there to "police" employee production. You must establish an adequate reporting measure for employee production. Use of Basecamp, Google Docs, Dropbox, and daily, weekly, and monthly reporting is essential.
4. **Conduct in-person meetings**. Schedule at least a few days a year meeting and bonding in person. The key takeaway is that your virtual employees feel bonded with you and the company.

***Lesson: Treat virtual employees well, and they can be productivity powerhouses!***

Other tools Mike mentions for your virtual company are TripIt, Drupalize.ME, Tech Stipend, Let's Freckle, The Lullabot Field Guide, Lockify, and TurboBridge.

Koa Hills Consulting is headquartered in Hawaii. The team is spread throughout the United States. Daily communication is most commonly conducted through videoconferencing and chat. Team collaboration on projects is achieved through a cloud-based document storage system. Employees collaborate from client sites, home offices, smart devices, and often from the tarmac. There really are no limitations.

The primary obstacles of managing and growing a virtual company are communication breakdowns, less personal interaction, multiple time zones, complexity of projects, and multiple reporting relationships. All of these can be overcome with good strategic planning and management.

When running a virtual company, communication is even more critical than when running a traditional company, simply due to the fact that you and your employees are *not* in the same office space. This means that you will be leveraging phone, text, chat, e-mail, and videoconferencing such as Google Hangouts. This can become overwhelming without some strategic ground rules around the use of these tools. It is not helpful for *everyone* to be copied on every e-mail message, and on the other end of the spectrum, it may not be prudent to communicate important company-wide information through a text.

Between Mike's Tuesday and Thursday lectures, he drove his rental car to Bend, Oregon, to do a presentation on using tools to conduct business remotely. The irony was not lost on Mike. He also tells a story to the class that gave them great insight into the demands of running your own business. Mike had completed an exhausting two-week road trip and was scheduled to fly home to his family on Sunday. While at SFO, he received a request to give a personal proposal to Scripps Research Institute on Monday. He changed flight reservations, flew to San Diego, made his presentation, and received a very lucrative contract.

***Lesson: You'd better have a high energy level and an exceptional ability to multitask.***

Mike's lectures were extremely valuable to the students. Many of them will go on to run a virtual company. All of them will have to master social media.

13

# Axioms, Heresy, and Closure: Best Practices, Dogmas, and the End Game

W. Gary Sitton

Over the course of my career, I developed twenty-two business axioms. These have been published in a few places and are used today by a very successful author and corporate consultant, Marsha Petrie Sue. I think each of these would qualify as a ***Lesson.*** These were presented to the class.

***Axiom #1: Make more coffee when you leave less than a cup.*** The basic message here is try not to hire lazy or thoughtless people. Both of these characteristics are a huge negative in a company in terms of morale and dollars.

***Axiom #2: The first six people you hire will set the work, social, ethical, and intellectual character of your company; be extremely careful with these hires.*** We were so fortunate with the first hires. I had the advantage of knowing them as students, and I could sense a strong character with each of them. It is interesting that in all the years I ran Bi-Tech, I only fired four people. However, many left. In order to become productive, new employees had to learn the software. In order to do this, you need help. If a new hire showed work habits or ethical or intellectual character values that did not mesh with the other employees, he or she simply would get no help and would leave, rather quickly. The record was four hours. I hired a programmer; he came to work at 8:00 a.m., left for lunch, and never returned. I called him at home and asked what was wrong. He said,

"You work too hard." Another major reason for our early success is that I wouldn't interview you if you had less than a 3.5 GPA, and I always asked to see the transcripts. We relaxed this requirement as we grew.

***Axiom #3: Understand, respect, trust, and celebrate what your employees do for you.*** Employees truly enjoy working where they are appreciated. Bi-Tech had the lowest employee turnover rate in our industry. In our business, we sold large systems to highly visible clients. As they got to know our employees, they wanted to hire them. In our industry, if you don't like your job, you can go across the street and get another one.

***Axiom #4: Be honest with your employees, even when it hurts.*** There were a few times where we had to call everyone together to tell them we were having cash-flow issues. Luckily, we got through those times. Another thing we did that helped our retention was making our books available 24/7, online, to every employee. At any time, they could look at our balance sheet and income statement, using IFAS, of course. Obviously, we did not give access to detailed payroll information. The one time I was not forthright with our employees was during the acquisition. I waited until the acquisition was 99 percent complete. I feared their reaction; in hindsight, I probably could have been open about it.

***Axiom #5: Never borrow money.*** This only applied to us. My view was if we can't make more than we spend, we shouldn't be in business; and borrowing money burdens your company with debt. Fact is there are many very successful companies that fund their growth with debt; Sierra Nevada Brewing is a case in point.

***Axiom #6: Don't confuse being smart with having a knack for something.*** I found this to be a most interesting axiom. There are simply some people who are really good at certain things. Your job as a leader is to discover who is good at what.

***Axiom #7: Encourage employees with a negative attitude to work for your competitors.*** Nothing is more damaging to a company than having an employee with a negative attitude. They give rise to strife, mistrust, and reduced productivity.

***Axiom #8: Let employees make important decisions and mistakes (you've got to do both).*** When employees get to make critical decisions, they feel engaged and valuable. The value of engagement far outweighs the risk of mistakes; and over the years, the employees got it right about as much as I did.

***Axiom #9: Hire a few people who tease and cut up (they keep things light).*** Your employees will spend 30-plus percent of their life at your company. Having a light atmosphere helps make them feel good about being at work. Sometimes our practical jokes got a little out of hand. When we were working out of the A-frame, we had a springer spaniel that was nuts for a flashlight beam. Ray Kaminski (someone who clearly matched this axiom) took a tea towel and tied a flashlight to the dog's head. We had beautiful herringbone redwood siding inside one of the rooms. The dog would see the light beam on the siding and attack. Judy came into the room and saw all the scratches; she was not amused.

***Axiom #10: Listen carefully to your clients; they will tell you how to stay in business.*** The close relationship we established with our clients was invaluable to getting feedback on how we were doing. Having our clients draw up a list of enhancements to our software kept us very competitive.

***Axiom #11: Leave your office door unlocked and open.*** With the exception of my conference calls with Frank Diehl and employees who were having personal problems, my office door was never shut, never locked. I kept all my private documents, like payroll information, in a locked file cabinet in my office. I thought it was important for an employee to walk by my office and just step in to chat.

***Axiom #12: Minimize company policy and procedures.*** There is no policy or procedure statement that will keep jerks from being jerks. Treat people like adults, and they will generally act like adults.

***Axiom #13: Honor all contracts.*** This axiom is a major reason we were never involved in litigation of any form.

***Axiom #14: Undercommit and overdeliver.*** Okay, this is the one with which we had the most trouble. In the early years, while striving for a contract, we sometimes relaxed this axiom. Without exception, violating this axiom brought regret.

***Axiom #15: Family comes first; work comes second.*** This was a big part of the company character. It really started when seventeen employees were working out of the A-frame with our two kids running around. If a family had a crisis, we did everything we could to help. This philosophy was also part of SunGard. When my son died, they told me to take as much time as I needed.

***Axiom #16: The best committee size is one.*** For some projects, such as a complete rewrite of the package, this doesn't work. I have found great success over the years by assigning one person to a development task and then leaving him or her alone to complete it. Because one person invests his or her ego into the task, the outcome is typically better than expected. People enjoy doing important work on their own.

***Axiom #17: Get paid for your work.*** This was pounded into me by SunGard. When we were acquired, Phil Dowd, my bosses' boss, put a plaque on my desk that said, "Get Paid for Your Work." Fact is, if you charge for your work, the client values it more.

***Axiom #18: Take time to chat with employees.*** This follows the "management by walking around" theory. It works. You don't always have to talk about work.

***Axiom #19: Anyone can be replaced.*** Judy and I were, and the company is doing fine today, fourteen years after we retired.

***Axiom #20: Don't let attorneys tell you how to run your business.*** When I was with the Statewide Academic Senate, I got to meet John O'Connell. John was a Chico State engineering graduate and went on to be president of Bechtel Corporation, a huge international enterprise. While I was contemplating starting Bi-Tech, I had a chance to sit down with John and ask him some questions. One of my questions was, "What is your view of attorneys?" John said, "You can use them to keep you out of trouble or get you out of trouble; I prefer the latter."

***Axiom #21: Employee turnover is much more expensive than paying well.*** We paid our employees very well. That's a very big reason they stayed with us.

***Axiom #22: Never, ever, think you have figured out how to run a successful business.*** Being a lifelong learner helps you stay in business.

## Heresy

Throughout the course of my life, I have made some dogmatic statements that would have been better left unsaid. These were presented to the class.

***Dogma #1: After seeing my father fail in four businesses, I swore I would never have my own business.*** My dad had two grocery stores and two bars; the stores went out of business, and the bars did him in. I was extremely hesitant to start my own business.

***Dogma #2: I will never write accounting software; it's boring, you know.*** Well, it turned out writing accounting software was pretty good for me.

***Dogma #3: I might start my own company, but I will never hire employees.*** When the system took off, I learned otherwise. You can't do it all yourself.

***Dogma #4: I will never move this company from my house.*** When the employee count hit seventeen, I had no choice.

***Dogma #5: We don't need documentation specialists; programmers can write user guides.*** Truth is, some can and some can't.

***Dogma #6: We don't need trainers; programmers can train people to use the software.*** It turns out this is not a good use of a programmer's time.

***Dogma #7: We don't need to hire accountants; programmers can learn accounting.*** When installing a complex system at a client's site, they want a "real" accountant to assist them.

***Dogma #8: I'll never have a marketing department; I can sell stuff.*** The significant growth of our company came only after I hired people in marketing and sales.

***Dogma #9: We don't need a quality assurance department; programmers can test their own code.*** Programmers, even good ones, lack the skill to stress-test code like real clients. For every bug you fix before release, it costs you $1; after release, $10 (sometimes much more). It pays to stress-test your software.

***Dogma #10: We don't need a help desk; programmers can solve problems clients are having with the system.*** Once again, this is not a good use of a programmer's time; and not all programmers are good with helping users of the software.

***Dogma #11: We don't need a personnel department; Judy and I can hire everyone.*** This was true in the beginning; however, when we reached eighty employees, we were spending most of our time with personnel issues. This was not a good use of Judy's and my time.

***Dogma #12: We will never need an internal accountant to do our books; the office manager and I can keep the books.*** With growth came a concomitant increase in company transactions, and we simply couldn't keep up.

***Dogma #13: We will never sell Bi-Tech.*** No comment required here.

***Lesson: Avoid dogmatic statements that may become heresy.***

## Closure

Three goals of the class (and thus this book) were to inform, excite, and engage. I assembled a very solid group of guest lecturers who could clearly and candidly inform the students about business lessons that can be successfully applied to a startup or a going concern. Hopefully the excitement of starting and running a business comes through the chapters. As for getting engaged, that is up to you. You have seen what it takes to run a business and the level of energy, luck, stress, and sometimes heartache that goes with it. Would I go back and do it all over again? *You bet!*

# Appendix 1

# Demonstrations

My nephew, Mike Monroe, wanted to do software demonstrations at the company I founded. Mike has been a successful trainer and consultant with the company, violating the adage "Don't hire relatives." Someone recommended Mike come talk to me because I did hundreds of demos, some of which turned out okay. Mike called me and asked if I could meet with him sometime in the next couple of weeks. We set a meeting for the next week, and I began to think about what I would tell the kid. (He is actually a full-grown man with a family and one daughter doing her MD residency, but I still think of him as a kid.)

As I thought about each little aspect of doing a demo, I decided to write down some notes. As often happens, some notes turned into many notes. So, for what it's worth, here is my diatribe on doing demos from 2007. Mike knows how Uncle Gary talks, so I wrote this like a letter to Mike, not the way I would write an academic paper. I also seriously violated my "keep it under a page" theory of business communications. Keep in mind, much of this is transferable to other demonstrations not related to software.

## Who Does Great Demos?

A complete, detailed knowledge of all the software you are going to show is a good start. Develop a keen understanding of the jobs performed by the people who need the software. Break yourself of any annoying mannerisms (like saying "um" a lot, scratching your balls, or using poor

English). Be polite and respectful, no matter how much you want to throttle the person asking you a dumb question. Attend as many demos from other people as you can stand. It is extremely important to develop your own style and approach—that is, don't try to be someone you're not. I have seen great demo persons who are grossly overweight, too ugly for words, too pretty to be liked by other women, too handsome to be liked by other men, lacked a sense of humor, dressed like slobs, and a myriad of other qualities you might think wouldn't work for a great demo person.

On top of my desk, I kept a list of every employee (> 200 when I retired). At least once a month, I would go over every name on the list and think of who might do good demos. You would be amazed at some of the people "types" who turned out to be great. You would also be amazed at some of the "most likely to succeed" who turned out to be complete demo duds. I still think there are untried people in that company who would be great.

Beyond the essential detailed knowledge of the software, there are just three characteristics that seem consistent in great demo people:

1. They have some way to establish credibility quickly in front of a crowd.
2. They enjoy being the center of attention.
3. They hate to lose.

You can't teach 2 and 3, but there are some things you can do about 1. Credibility is, simply put, the audience's belief that you have real-world experience and you are a truth teller. The experience part can come from credentials (e.g., CPA), from development experience, from training and consulting experience, from help-desk experience, from quality assurance experience, or from working in an institution similar to that of your prospective client. You are in control of the truth-teller part. My advice is to be one. There are also a few people who just exude confidence and people believe that they are credible, no matter what their background is. I don't know much about these kinds of people, but I secretly hope they get caught.

## Preparation

The more you know about a given prospective client, the better you will do. Use the Internet to research the prospect. Make phone calls to people who are going to be watching you. Say, "I'm going to be showing you our software and want to know if there is anything particular you would like me to include?" This question usually gives rise to other dialogue and helps you find out who the key decision makers are and what their hot buttons are. Be sure and ask what it is about their current system that bugs them. Take good notes on your conversations. Remember their names so you can chat with them about the call during your breaks. With that information, you can say, "In our call, you wanted me to include 'x.' Are you okay with 'x' now?"

Once you have determined who the decision makers are, you should have a demo strategy. You can't always know who the decision makers are. I did quite different demos if the IT department was going to make the decision and would focus more on the "techie" side and talk about how updates and security are handled, modular design methodology, and all the buzzwords for the day. If the accountants were the drivers, I would use lots of T-accounts and focus on month- and year-end closing and reporting processes. If payroll/personnel were driving the decision, I would grind up the applicant-to-retirement flow into a fine dust.

If the selection involves an RFP, as most do, review the response before you do the demo. Pay close attention to the "evaluation criteria" stated in the RFP. These contain giant clues on what's important and lets you "teach to the test." Don't go into the demo without first doing a run-through on the "demo box." You would be amazed at some of the stuff I found on the demo system just before the opening dialogue. Ray Kaminski used to put embarrassing common codes out there just to provoke my ire.

While on the topic of the demo box, look at it as the way for you to make this demo look like it was tailor-made for the prospective client. If they had scripts in the RFP, check out each one. Make sure you set their name in as the client and do as much client-specific setup as possible. The more you make it look like their system, the better they will like it. Don't be afraid to use a little colloquial humor when doing your setup, for example, "Jane's Impossible Benefits Calculation" for a calc-code title will draw positive attention during the demo.

## Getting There

Before you leave on the trip, double-check that you have everything you will need. Gary Wolz and I flew the Archer down to Los Angeles to do a demo. We touched down about half an hour before sunrise. As we were unloading the plane, I asked Gary where the demo tape was; this was back when we used magnetic tape and had to install the system before the demo. Gary gave me a blank stare and said, "I thought you put it in." After several expletives, a call was placed to Don Carlos, the IT director at the Claremont Colleges, a client. We took a cab to Claremont, cut a tape, raced to the prospect site, Dominguez Hills Foundation, and the demo started on time, barely. That was when I decided maybe it would be a good idea to double-check that everything was packed.

## Physical Appearance

In the movies, villains have beards. I've known one really good demo person, Mike Fox, who had a beard and was successful; that's one among many. Unless you're doing the "techie" part of the demo, I advise no beard; or if you must, have it well-groomed. Mustaches, okay, but now we're splitting hairs (pun intended).

Generally your wardrobe should be "appropriate business attire," whatever that might be by today's standards; probably not what I wear every day. I learned an interesting thing about appearance while giving a demo to Beeville College in Beeville, Texas. Since I was traveling to that part of the world, I wore my cowboy boots and Levi's on the plane. My checked luggage got lost, so I did the demo in my travel clothes. I opened by telling them my travel woes and apologizing for not being in "appropriate business attire." It normally takes about two hours to see the audience relax and start rooting for you, but these Beevillians were in my pocket in ten minutes. From time to time, when I thought it might help, I would "have trouble finding my checked luggage."

One other thing I always did right before I left my hotel room was look in the mirror and say out loud, "One hundred percent; no defects." I know, it's kind of stupid, but for some reason, this made me feel confident, not cocky. This is a good way to focus before you do a demo.

## Setup

First, in advance of the date the demo will happen, find out how many will be in the audience, what building and room will be used, where you should park, and who is going to meet you first on the day of the demo. Also, try to have everybody there for the overview and the wrap-up. Make sure you give yourself maximum setup time. I used to call the prospect and ask how early someone could let me in the room. If I couldn't get an answer to my "how early" question, I would show up early and look for someone in Security to let me into the room. Once in the room, get the lighting correctly set. Find out where the switches are and if they have rheostats, look at the windows and consider where the sun will be during the demo, and then find some way to cover the windows if there will be too much ambient light. It is very frustrating to have trouble seeing the projected images. A frustrated audience is not a happy audience.

Once you get the room lighting organized, boot up the system. Don't forget to take some long extension cords. Fill the screen; bigger is better. Don't forget to take an extra projector bulb with you. In fact, extra everything is a good idea. Now that the lighting and system are set up, do the seating so that every seat in the house is a good one, and you have room to prance around with your laser pointer without standing in someone's way. After all that, put out the doughnuts and coffee. Yes, this is a very important part of having a happy audience. Do a quick software run-through before your audience arrives, just to make sure things are working. If not, get people out of bed to help you.

## Opening Dialogue

That first half an hour of overview is the most important part of the demo. You have limited time to hit the hot buttons, show them something with a gee-whiz factor, establish personal credibility, establish company credibility, and get the audience thinking maybe they will like you. The major key to credibility is to be known as a truth teller.

One line I used quite often in the opening dialogue was, "There are parts of this package that are extremely well-thought-out and easy to use. There are also parts that are klutzy and hard to use. As I go through the various subsystems, I will point out both parts." Then, with each subsystem, I would point out at least one "minor" flaw that I felt should be addressed in the software—something like, "This is a three-step process, and it should be simplified into a one-step process."/ Or, "It seems to take a heck of a lot of setup to get the work flow defined properly. Of course, once you have it in place, it does save steps and avoids bottlenecks." Having the demo person point out weaknesses makes them seem like little things that just need to be addressed. Leaving them unsaid or unaddressed makes them seem like big problems. Also, if you point out a problem, note, if it's true, that it's currently under review to incorporate into the package.

## Humor

If you possess a good sense of humor, by all means blend it into your demo. Getting people to laugh puts them at ease, and it makes them want to root for you. I found that self-debasing humor worked best for me. Telling an embarrassing story about yourself rarely offends others. Humor relating to race, religion, gender, sex, politics, cultural groups, sports, music, and the like is pretty risky. Improvisational humor based on the context of a question or circumstance, while my favorite type of humor, can also be pretty risky.

It is also pretty important to see the humor embedded in the life of a demo person. Lots of funny things happen out there on the road. My most embarrassing moment came while doing a demo for Trinity Christian College, north of Chicago. The day started out bad, as the entire college lost electricity. For two hours in a very dark room, I basically had to entertain them without a demo system. When the power came on, I had to do major catch-up, but it started going quite well. There were lots of good questions, and they liked all the answers. I could see and feel the audience relax, become friendly, and start to root for me. You know they are rooting for you when people in the audience help you answer questions.

I always do a break right before the wrap-up, so people can focus on my last words and not be thinking about how badly they want to use the restroom. I made a quick trip to the men's room and returned for the wrap-up. I started by asking if anyone had questions about what they had seen; dead silence was the response. It was as if someone had turned off a switch. I thought maybe they had all heard some horrible news during the break, because the pallor over the audience was epic. I resorted to my usual wrap-up talk, packed up my gear, got into my rental car, and started driving south to O'Hare Airport.

There was a lot of snow on the ground, and I spotted some white-tailed deer on the side of the freeway. You know, I'm always looking for deer. When I looked over at them, something else appeared in my peripheral vision. I was wearing a three-piece suit and a pink shirt—acceptable attire in the eighties. When I had finished relieving myself at the urinal during the last break, I had zipped the tail of my shirt so that about three inches of it was sticking straight out of the top of my fly. I can remember turning crimson red, followed by laughing until my sides hurt. I still laugh when I think about it. Trinity did not become a client, but I bet they still tell the story about the weirdo from California.

## Questions

Audience questions are the very best opportunity you will be given to shine. This is where your in-depth knowledge of the software can make you into a hero. First, even though you know the answer immediately, take just a couple of seconds to quietly think about the question. This lets them know you take their questions seriously, and it makes them more likely to listen to your answer. The pre-answer pause is way more effective than saying, "That's a good question," which everyone knows is BS.

You will get questions that leap over the stupid border. Generally, most of the people in the room know it's a stupid question. Remember that we all ask stupid questions from time to time, and we appreciate an accurate, polite, and respectful answer.

You will also get questions to which you do not know the answer. Say, "I don't know the answer to that question." Then, write it down and write down the person's name. Let them see you write it down. Don't tell them you'll get back to them because they won't believe it. Rather, when you get back home, send them the answer, if you find it out.

An effective demo person will use questions posed to the audience. Learn the names of people in your audience. Write names down and make a seating chart if you have to. Address questions directly to individuals by name. For example, "Fred, where in the work flow do you encumber a PO?" Ask questions that can lead you into showing some of the best parts of the software, without having it look like you are setting someone up to be your straight man. Questions from the audience are a great springboard for you to ask questions of the audience. Don't ask the audience a question that they may not be able to answer. They like answering questions.

## Problem Systems

Unless the world has changed dramatically since I was doing demos, you can count on having some problems with the system during almost every demo. The hardware, connection, or software will fail, typically the software. This is where you need to be the "iceman," showing no concern whatsoever. Understand that 99 percent of the time, nobody in the audience knows you are having a problem. Dan Terrell is the master at this. I have watched him do demos where the software was dying left and right, and Dan's fingers would be flying across the keyboard as if everything that was going on was exactly as he expected. He didn't even break stride on what he was talking about.

There will be times where you just have to call a time-out to fix something. Be direct about it with your audience by saying something like, "I'm going to need some time to chase down a problem I'm having. If you will all sit quietly and not stare at me too much, I'll try to get it fixed quickly." If you need more than a few minutes, tell them, "Mill around because this is going to take more than a few minutes." Never send them back to their offices because several will not return.

## Problem People

It is unusual to do a demo where there are no "problem people." Most people who are a problem during a demo are not well-liked by their peers. Here are some suggestions of how to handle these folks.

The "can't shut up" person: This creates problems because you can't get through your demo material. During the first break, I try to take this person aside and say something like, "You seem to have a lot more questions and comments than most people I run into. Many of the things you say interest me, but I have to get through my material and this demo is my only shot. Would you mind cutting back on the comments so I can get through my stuff?" Another approach is to tell the audience you will leave ten minutes at the end of each segment for questions. Personally, I don't like this approach, but sometimes it's the only effective way to deal with someone who can't shut up.

The "I hate software vendors" person: If the person is overt, I just deal with it straight up by saying something like, "I can see you have had huge problems with vendors. It's probably because you've been sold a bill of goods, received rotten service, had terrible implementation experiences, or tried to use software that doesn't work most the time, or all of the above. If you'll just lighten up on me a little, I'll do my level best not to sell you a bill of goods." For the less overt types, see comments above on stupid questions.

The "I heard ..." person: Anytime you hear a comment start out with this, plant your feet because you're about to be put on the spot. For example, "I heard your help desk gives rotten service." You better have a reasonable and believable response ready. Something like, "You know, most of the people who work the help desk used to be trainers who grew tired of travel. They know the software inside-out, and they really care about problems people are having. Our help desk takes over 'x' calls each month, and some of the problems we tackle are extremely complex because they deal with people like you who have extremely complex jobs. Out of all the calls we take, I have no doubt that some of them could be handled quicker or better; but know this, every call and resolution is logged into a database, carefully reviewed each day, and we take no aspect of this business more seriously than we do support." As you begin to collect your "I heard ..." list, prepare the best possible response. And don't forget to pass the "I heard ..." list back to the company.

The "I'm smarter than you" person: Play to such people. They have huge egos, and there is nothing you can do to change that. As long as they don't morph into the "can't shut up" group, let them have their day in the sunshine. You'll get even when the contract gets signed.

## Breaks

Have lots of them. Some of the most effective selling happens during a break, where you can get to know some of the people in a conversational setting. Don't be afraid to talk about things that have nothing to do with software and support. Have at least one break an hour, if it is approved by the prospective client. People just can't stay focused or enthused for long periods of time without a break. And you need some time to reflect on how things are going and where things should be going. When you give a break, tell the audience when it will be over (e.g., five minutes) and then stick to it.

## Wrap-Up

At the end of each demo, you are given approximately fifteen to thirty minutes for wrap-up. Customize this based on how the demo has gone. If it has gone really well, just use it as a question-and-answer time; they like that better than a hard sell. If you're not sure how well it has gone, develop a monologue that speaks to what you think is most important in their decision. This is also a good time to ask the prospective client what else they need to make an evaluation. If you know it has gone badly, don't be afraid to say so and ask them if they could give you some pointers on improvement. People are amazingly generous when you meet them halfway.

## Going On or Going Home

There are going to be times when you are out on the road and you get sick. Airplane rides provide maximum viral exposure. Doing a demo is like being in a Broadway play, only you don't have an understudy in the wings. When you think you can't go on, think about all the preparation and thousands of hours and dollars that have led up to this opportunity. If you still think you can't go on, go home. In my twenty-five years, I missed one day of work because I couldn't stay out of the bathroom. I never missed a demo due to illness—airplanes, yes; illness, no. I'm proud of that, and I know I may have given hundreds of people the flu, but I never missed a demo.

## Follow-Up

When you get home or back to your hotel room, prepare a follow-up strategy. Get answers to questions you couldn't answer. Schedule or make phone calls to prospects, time zones permitting. Handwrite a few thank-you notes to individuals you liked or you wish liked you better. Make a few entries in your personal journal about what you learned, what worked well and what didn't; when you retire, you can write a book. Send an e-mail back to the marketing and sales folks telling them how it went, what you think they can do to help sell it, and any other tidbits that will improve your chances of a win.

## Postmortem

Of the two things that can happen, win and lose, the latter is the one from which you learn the most. Unfortunately, people are always happy to tell you why you won, but hesitant to tell you why you lost. Call them anyway and tell them, "Losing is like taking castor oil—first it makes you sick and then it makes you better." Let them know they are doing you a huge favor by sharing this information. Take good notes on what they tell you; then share the wealth with the company.

## Make the Company Better

As the person doing the demo, you are on the front lines. All the training, BS, strategy, and planning are out the window as you get down to a real-world challenge. You will be the first to find out what people want, like, don't want, don't like, and don't care about. You do a great service to your company by bringing back this information. Your company does a great service to you by taking action on your issues. The best information I ever learned about what the package should be doing came from doing demos, listening to what real people want, and then finding a way for the software to do it.

## Some Don'ts

Don't go on and on about your prior jobs. It's boring, and it makes people afraid you think their organization is like the place(s) you used to work. It's not.

Don't talk badly about the competition. If a prospective client backs you into a corner and asks you to comment on company "x", say, "My job is to represent my company; your job is to select the best company to meet your needs. All these companies have user groups. I give you my strongest encouragement to get a list of users and call every one of them. Ignore the client reference list unless you know every client is on it. Ask the vendor for a list of every client to whom they have sold software in the last twelve months. Call them. Find out about any past or pending litigation; your attorneys can do this. Use your user group list to find out who stopped using the vendor's products. Call them. I could probably dredge up some hearsay, embellish it, and say something scathing about all the other vendors. Fact is, they are all pretty good companies, trying their best to keep old clients and attract new ones. The only thing I will tell you about company 'x' is I knew about them when I was looking for a job that met my needs."

Don't beat yourself up when you do badly. To quote Aunt Judy, "Regret is the cancer of life." Sometimes you're just not "on." Learn from it and then forget about it.

Don't be lazy about preparation and follow-up.

Don't let it eat at you when the company can't or won't fix issues you know about. There are never enough people in a software company to address all issues, and there is always way more demand than supply. The single most important thing your company can do for itself, its clients, and you is stay in business. This requires some manufactured equilibrium among development, implementations, consultants, documentation, R & D, quality assurance, help desk, computer center management, accounting, corporate reporting, community service, and marketing and sales. Trust me, I did it for twenty-five years; it's not easy, and you never know if you have manufactured the best equilibrium.

Don't be afraid to surprise your audience. If your demo is going quite well, slip in some interesting and surprising PowerPoint slides (or whatever the latest demo medium happens to be). I would occasionally slip in slides of monster fish I caught and released. As you might guess, I avoided all the slides of animals I killed. For the Cousteau Society, I even took the "dead heads" (as Aunt Judy calls them) out of my office.

## Closing Diatribe

As you go through developing your own style and approach and learn what works and what doesn't work for you, keep track of your wins and losses in a personal journal. Reflect on them often. Never, ever, think you are the best you can be. The dynamics of doing a software demonstration in front of strangers are ever-changing, and being good at it means you become a student of it, always learning. Being good at doing demos is both a gift and an acquired skill. And it is important work. Being second is the pits. Winning is a rush. And unlike professional athletics, you never get too old or too lame to play.

As a demo person, you will have many treasured memories. There were many wins (and losses) that I will never forget. My most agonizing loss: City of Oakland. This was when we were just starting to show our software to really large clients. We went through a very demanding RFP and did several software demonstrations. We were notified that we had won; then, a few weeks later, we were told we were not selected. Turned out one of our competitors was fairly active in campaign funding for the city council. I was crestfallen.

My favorite win: Fairbanks Northstar Borough. Once again, we had a fairly major RFP. I was the last one to demo after PeopleSoft, Oracle, and AMS. By the way, I believe last is always best, if you can get it. It was a two-day demo. As soon as the lights were dimmed and the projector turned on, someone in the front row asked where our "team" was. I said I didn't understand the question, and the person said PeopleSoft brought ten people, Oracle brought eight people, and I can't remember how many people she said AMS brought. I explained that I knew all the software pretty well, and there would be no other people from Bi-Tech. Man, was it ever fun to kick the competition's butts in that demo! I really liked those people up there because they were good, hardworking, and honest people.

# Appendix 2

# Lessons

## Preface Lessons

- *We tend not to perform well if we don't have some skin in the game.*

## Chapter 1 Lessons: Birth, Growth, and Acquisition of a Software Company, W. Gary Sitton

- *Sometimes, taking a chance on someone pays off.*
- *You'd be surprised what you can do when you've found your niche.*
- *Sometimes you need a bit of luck and a lot of patience.*
- *Software languages come and go.*
- *Don't stay with a bad thesis supervisor or mentor.*
- *When you are nervous, don't put the cup on a saucer.*
- *The perfect time to have kids seldom appears.*
- *Treat each job as a training experience for your next job.*
- *If you're going to sell software, you need clear title.*
- *Don't rely on the secretary of state to search your company's name.*
- *Always be on the lookout for a great employee.*
- *There's a right way and a wrong way to pirate your clients' employees.*
- *Diversity of vertical markets can help you withstand downturns.*
- *If you are going to have a user group, let the users control it.*
- *If you are looking to be acquired, prepare a list of requirements.*
- *When given the option of money or stock, consult experts before deciding.*
- *Careful crafting can create a very flexible software package.*

## Chapter 2 Lessons: Marketing and Sales, Drake Brown

- *Knowing all the roles of marketing will help you grow your business.*
- *The earlier you can disqualify a prospect, the more success you will have.*
- *Selling is a process.*
- *Become a student of the sales funnel and sales forecast.*
- *Trust is earned through honesty.*
- *If the fit's not good, walk.*
- *Try to find a coach.*
- *It does you no good to horse-trade if you're out of horses.*
- *With some of your demonstrations, you need to pull out all the stops.*
- *Being careful with even small expenditures is important in a startup business.*
- *Don't spend any energy making excuses when you goof.*
- *Shower employees with caring and make them feel part of the family.*
- *Treating your employees with kindness is always a great investment.*
- *Surprise your employees now and then (when they deserve it) and see what they will do for you.*
- *Blunt honesty gives rise to a partnership.*

## Chapter 3 Lessons: Human Resources, Kristi Bennett

- *Be specific in your contract with independent contractors.*
- *Know what classifies a worker as an independent contractor.*
- *When in doubt, classify as nonexempt.*
- *Inaccurate exempt classification can cost your company money.*
- *Keep accurate records of nonexempt employees.*
- *Interview standards can help avoid litigation.*
- *The formal job offer must clearly state many details.*
- *The first day on the job should be well planned and informed.*
- *Make sure your employee postings are complete; it is the law.*
- *A paper trail can save you.*
- *Personnel issues require common sense.*
- *Keep good documentation and make fair employment decisions.*

## Chapter 4 Lessons: Customer Service and Employee Recognition, Judy Sitton

- *It's important that your employees act as client advocates.*
- *Explore and develop your passions in life; the outcome will bring great personal happiness and satisfaction.*
- *RATER should be top-of-mind in providing exceptional service.*
- *Without trust, the customer/vendor relationship will be a dismal failure.*
- *Listening with focus will enhance your customer/vendor experience.*
- *Positive words/phrases set the tone for productive service communication.*
- *Your mood comes through a call;* smile—*they can hear it in your voice.*
- *Pay attention to both verbal and nonverbal cues to ensure exceptional customer communication.*
- *Thankfulness is at the heart of true appreciation for ourselves and others. Be grateful and express it!*
- *Never underestimate the power and positive effect of an apology.*
- *Recognition is more than the icing on the cake—it's the whole cake!*

## Chapter 5 Lessons: Research and Development, James Bennett

- *Never forget you are there to solve a problem.*
- *Never pass up a real-world perspective.*
- *Hire exceptional people, regardless of their degree.*
- *Beware of short-term employment goals.*
- *Always assess the indirect cost of an employee.*
- *Your current project is a training ground for your next project.*
- *Be a "Yes,* and *..." employee.*
- *The frequency of communication is a function of distance.*
- *When meeting remotely, include the meeting after the meeting.*
- *The acquiring company cares about EBIDTA, not synergy.*
- *A steering committee can help defuse culture clashes.*
- *Time-zone differences can take two days for a five-minute conversation.*
- *Dialect training can help with offshore communications.*
- *Recruitment in India takes longer, and they have different holidays.*

- *Cultural-awareness training actually helps.*
- *Your solution involves your code,* plus *a great deal more.*
- *Technical debt is an inevitable outcome of product development.*
- *You must schedule realistic estimates to address technical-debt issues.*
- *Software options are confusing, expensive, and difficult to support.*
- *Cloud development wins; however, understand the SLA (service-level agreement) and get advice on data privacy.*
- *Internal policies need to keep pace with internal approval requirements.*
- *An API and scripting help savvy users, not the help desk.*
- *Examine all methods to detect and report errors.*

## Chapter 6 Lessons: The CFO Duties, Bruce Langston

- *Find what you're good at and stick with it.*
- *Recognize opportunity and jump on it.*
- *Management is a key ingredient to employee retention and a successful business.*
- *If you don't like where you are, move on.*
- *Sometimes you need to test yourself on a bigger stage.*
- *Silos can be deadly to a company.*
- *A company's management structure is not a democracy.*
- *Don't rely or count on miracles.*
- *Budgeting and forecasting are a team effort.*
- *In business, almost nothing goes according to plan.*
- *Revenue recognition policy is critical.*
- *The balance sheet, over time, can show the health of the company.*
- *Be well-prepared for an acquisition.*
- *Never, ever, carry over a balance on a credit card.*
- *Depending on your business, you may want to use asset-based lending.*

## Chapter 7 Lessons: Business Realities, Mark Fitzpatrick

- *There are a lot of bored, angry, smart people with massive amounts of computing horsepower at their fingertips.*
- *People are visual and generally pretty impatient when it comes to software.*

- *For most products, people like to be sold if you have value and you make the process fun and engaging.*
- *Leveraging the appropriate social-media platforms for your space can pay huge dividends and doesn't take a massive amount of work or money.*
- *If you don't get comfortable with the cloud, chances are you won't get far.*
- *Your software can kill somebody.*
- *Most startups don't put enough thought and resources into support; some recover and some don't.*
- *Lots of people can build software, but few can productize.*
- *Hiring developers in California is very, very expensive; great developers can be found overseas if you clearly specify what you want.*
- *Most trade shows are cheesy, but they can net huge dividends.*
- *Understand the risks of stock options.*
- *Don't be paranoid about sharing your idea.*
- Never *take money from FnF unless you warn them that they may* never, ever, *see the money again. If you don't succeed, there will* always *be a white elephant in the room with your ex-investors.*
- *Most VCs have great connections; unless you have real traction or an amazing track record, you aren't going to get VC funding.*
- *Always ask for advice and never ask for help.*
- *Being human is a good thing.*

## Chapter 8 Lessons: Global Sourcing and Startup Funding, Daren Otten

- *Know the risks of a project and have a backup plan.*
- *Lower labor costs can be found outside the United States.*
- *Try to negotiate payment terms more favorable than thirty days.*
- *The wage gap between the United States and offshore is decreasing.*
- *Reducing the transportation distance of completed products limits exposure to damage and reduces transportation cost.*
- *It is critical to look at the total production costs of a product.*
- *Currency exchange rates are volatile.*
- *Friends and family are often the first source for funding.*
- *Don't overlook the government as an initial funding source.*
- *There are alternative funding options.*

- *The Band of Angels awaits your proposal.*
- *Avoid stressful leveraged debt.*
- *When acquired or restructured, make sure personal liability is assigned to the new entity.*
- *To mitigate liability, restructure as you grow.*
- *A dry funding well is a red flag.*
- *Bankruptcy, while painful, need not be fatal.*
- *Your exit strategy should be reviewed annually or quarterly.*

## Chapter 9 Lessons: Finding Opportunity, Michael Reale

- *Always look for a better way to do something.*
- *Giving back to the community can become profitable.*
- *People can exhibit the entrepreneurial spirit in any endeavor they adopt, revenue-seeking or not.*
- *Few things in life are more fun than owning your own company.*
- *Before starting your startup, make sure you are* uniquely qualified.
- *Red oceans are good places to think about blue oceans.*

## Chapter 10 Lessons: International Commerce, Jessee Allread

- *Research is the key to international entrepreneurial efforts.*
- *Every country has a different way of doing business.*
- *Access and introductions are key elements in international business.*
- *Be on the lookout for new market segments.*
- *Never attend a trade show without set or scheduled appointments.*
- *Facebook and LinkedIn can help with introductions.*
- *Have an attorney draw up the contract with an in-country representative.*
- *Plan for product exchanges.*
- *Learn the business rules of your target country.*

## Chapter 11 Lessons: Project Management, Sean Morgan

- *If you're going to submit a bid, be on time.*
- *Project management is vision in action—that is,* execution.

- *Certified project managers make more money than those uncertified.*
- *Put the work in up front and avoid delays and budget overruns.*
- *Planning before you act is extremely important.*
- *As the project manager, be prepared to deal with conflict.*

## Chapter 12 Lessons: Social Media and the Virtual Company, Mike Monroe

- *Don't ignore postings on your Facebook page.*
- *Social media can be exploited to grow your business.*
- *Master social media; it's nearly free.*
- *Virtual teams = teams + electronic links + groupware.*
- *A virtual company has reduced overhead.*
- *Treat virtual employees well, and they can be productivity powerhouses!*
- *You'd better have a high energy level and an exceptional ability to multitask.*

## Chapter 13 Lessons: Axioms, Heresy, and Closure, W. Gary Sitton

- Each of the twenty-two axioms presented in this chapter would qualify as a ***Lesson***; take the time to go back and reread them.
- *Avoid dogmatic statements that may become heresy.*

# Bibliography

## References from the Book:

Anderson, Kristin, and Ron Zemke. *Delivering Knock Your Socks Off Service*. New York: AMACOM, 2011.

Boiney, Dr. Lindsley G. *Reaping the Benefits of Information Technology in Organizations: A Framework Guiding Appropriation of Group Support Systems*. The Journal of Applied Behavioral Science, 1998.

Burns, Kenneth, and Geoffrey C. Ward. *The Civil War*. New York: Knopf Publishing Group, 1994.

Collins, Jim. *Good to Great*. Williamsport, PA: Harper Collins, 2001.

Gladwell, Malcolm. *David and Goliath*. Boston, MA: Little, Brown and Company, 2013.

Gladwell, Malcolm. *Tipping Point*. Boston, MA: Little, Brown and Company, 2000.

Grossman, Ken. *Beyond the Pale*. Hoboken, NJ: Wiley, 2013.

Kidder, Tracy. *The Soul of a New Machine*. Oakland, CA: Locus Publications, 1982.

Kim, W. Chan, and Renee Mauborgne. *Blue Ocean Strategy*. Boston, MA: Harvard Business Press, 2005.

Nelson, Ted. *Home Computer Revolution*. Unknown: Distributors, 1978.

Post, Tom. *Startup Month: Entrepreneurs And Investors Weigh In On How To Launch A Business*, Forbes.Com., 2012.

Ries, Al, and Jack Trout. *The 22 Immutable Laws of Marketing*. Williamsport, PA: Harper Collins, 1994.

Spoonamore, Steve. *The Real Definition Of Entrepreneur—And Why It Matters*, Forbes, 2012.

Zhao, Yong. *World Class Learners*. Thousand Oaks, CA: SAGE Publications Inc., 2012.

## Other References You May Enjoy:

Blank, Steve. *The Four Steps to the Epiphany*. Raleigh, NC: Lulu Enterprises Incorporated, 2003.

Christensen, Clay. *The Innovator's Dilemma*. Boston, MA: Harvard Business Review Press, 1997.

Cooper, Brant, and Patrick Vlaskovits. *The Entrepreneurial Guide to Customer Development*. Unknown: CustDev, 2010.

Feld, Brad, and David Cohen. *Do More Faster*. Hoboken, NJ: Wiley, 2011.

Feld, Brad, and Jason Mendelson. *Venture Deals*. Hoboken, NJ: Wiley, 2013.

Fried, Jason, and David Heinemier Hannson. *Rework*. New York: Crown Publishing Group, 2010.

Graham, Paul. *Hackers and Painters*. New York: Penguin Books, 1994.

Hsieh, Tony. *Delivering Happiness*. Unknown: Grand Central Publishing, 2010.

Kawasaki, Guy. *The Art of the Start*. New York: Portfolio Hardcover, 2004.

Komisar, Randy. *The Monk and the Riddle*. Boston, MA: Harvard Business Press, 2001.

Ries, Eric. *Lean Startup*. New York: Crown Business, 2011.

Shapiro, Carl, and Hal Varian. *Information Rules*. Boston, MA: Harvard Business School Press, 1998.

Vaynerchuck, Gary. *The Thank You Economy*. New York: Harper Business, 2011.